Dramatic Techniques for Creative Writers

Turbo-Charge Your Writing

JULES HORNE

GW00659204

Ready to step your creative writing up a gear?
Discover the powerful dramatic secrets used by
industry storytelling professionals.

For writing tips, review copies and more,
join the mailing list at

www.method-writing.com

Texthouse, The Corn Exchange, Woodmarket, Kelso, TD5 7AT
www.texthouse.co.uk

Dramatic Techniques for Creative Writers: Turbo-Charge Your Writing
/ Jules Horne — 2nd ed.

Cover design: Victor Marcos
www.99designs.com/profiles/victormarcos/services

ISBN
978-0-9934354-9-2 (paperback)
978-1-9164960-0-2 (ebook)

Contents

vi

Is This You?

Are you an author who wants to take your craft to another level?
Are you a novelist, copywriter, scriptwriter or journalist keen to punch up your writing with powerful dramatic concepts?
Are you a playwriting or scriptwriting student who wants a grasp of key dramatic writing techniques?
A TV and film fan interested in writing skills?
A teacher of creative writing students?
Are you interested in dramatic writing secrets?

Join the Method Writing mailing list at
www.method-writing.com

Introduction

Writers! Do you want to write with more impact?

Then you've come to the right place.

This book is full of ideas to turbo-charge your writing craft.

They come from the world of drama.

They're the secrets playwrights, screenwriters for TV and film and radio dramatists use on a daily basis to create stories that work before an audience.

Secrets that other writers often don't know about.

Why do I know this?

OK, meet Kelly. She's an author. Let's say a friend. She's written plenty, had some of it published. Even won some prizes. She's published journalism, fiction, non-fiction, poetry – you name it. She can spin a sentence. She's great at grammar, an excellent self-editor. She knows her stuff.

One day, she goes along to a writing workshop to learn to write her first play. How hard can it be? she thinks. Characters speak stuff. You write it down. Maybe it's even quicker than fiction?

Oh boy. That day, Kelly learns that there's a whole new world out there. A world of writing techniques. A world of powerful writing concepts. Practical writing craft. Everything just as useful for fiction, non-fiction and poetry as for script.

And all completely new to her.

It's transformative.

Fast-forward a short while and Kelly's a changed writer, in her fiction, non-fiction and everything else.

She's wrangling scenes, secrets, action and dialogue with new confidence. She's creating dynamic characters that are driven, clear and engaging. She knows how to structure stories for maximum impact and momentum, and make tough editing choices far more quickly. She has a feel for story and sentence rhythm, and her writing has far more life.

And through it all, she thinks: Why didn't I *know* this? I'm a published author. This is dynamite. Why is it hidden from view?

And some of her thought: I could keep this all to myself. Because it was like discovering a secret stash of writing gold.

And then she wondered: Why don't dramatists share this gold? Maybe they want to keep it secret?

Then she realised: They don't often talk technique to other writers. So it stays in the industry bubble. A big shiny stash of writing gold, hidden in plain sight.

Then she decided to come clean and speak in the first person. Kelly is of course me, but she's thousands of other authors who have woken up to the power of dramatic techniques. People from fiction, screen, copywriting and journalism who are hungry for craft and want to write and edit at a higher level.

Writers are increasingly multimodal, and jump between print, web, script, podcasting, audiobooks and spoken word. Write for the ear and for performance as well as the eye. And more than that: they want to write boldly. With more impact.

In this book, I share what I've learned on my journey from writer to dramatic writer.

These craft skills have changed my fiction and non-fiction approach in powerful ways. They've given me new concepts for tackling any kind of writing with confidence. They've helped to speed up my planning, structuring and editing. They've got me writing commissions and given me an industry-level understanding of narrative technique.

I was unbelievably excited to discover these techniques. And at the same time baffled, because no one ever told me they existed. Even though I was an aspiring writer hungry to learn, I'd never encountered most of them.

This below-the-radar situation is starting to change. More and more, fiction writers are reading up on structure and dramaturgy, and passing on what they've learned about story, arcs, and dramatic action.

But there's plenty more gold to mine from the world of drama. Kelly has been the long way round:

- Endless dramaturgy workshops.
- Devouring books by Aristotle, McKee, Mamet, Vogler, Stanislavski, Marks, Aronson, Iglesias, Johnstone, Berne – all brimful of nuggets.
- A whole summer of reading Shakespeare, taking notes, asking: How does he *do* that? Not to mention other scriptwriters and great teachers.
- A deep-dive into narratology, psychology, discourse analysis, cognitive linguistics.
- Watching box sets, notebook in hand. Lots of box sets.
- Feeding back on hundreds of writers' works in progress, till my editorial skills are sharper than a Stanley knife.

And you're welcome to do all that, too!

Or you can cut to the chase, and simply read this book.

It includes the best nuggets from dramatic technique in clear, distilled form, so you can put them into action in your writing right away.

And a warning: It will transform the way you see films, TV, story and pretty well all human interaction. Are you ready? Let's go!

About Me

I'm an award-winning playwright and fiction writer, and I teach on a creative writing MA at a UK university.

Since I was tiny, I've loved reading, plays, films and stories. I've always written. I still love it more than anything else. And I still learn something new each day.

What's more unusual is that I'm multimodal. I write across different writing disciplines: scripts, fiction, journalism, web copy, poetry and lyrics. I've worked professionally in broadcast journalism, too. So, I've learned a wide range of writing techniques.

My writing mix includes fiction and over a dozen professional stage and BBC radio plays, two of them Edinburgh Fringe First winners.

I used to think being a multimodal writer was a problem. But now I realise it's ahead of the curve. The rise of the web, video and audiobooks means writing platforms are converging. The next generation of writers will be multimodal. In education, there are even conferences on the topic now.

So if you're like me and you're excited by the potential, this is a good place to start.

Why I Wrote This Book

I was sitting in a rehearsal room, with a group of experienced actors, and not the slightest clue about the foundations of dramatic writing.

It was my first script. I was a published fiction writer and journalist, but scriptwriting was new.

Story, characters, description, dialogue – sure. This was all familiar territory. I could weave a sentence, tell a story, make a character speak.

But people were using a completely different language to talk about the writing in front of us. Terms like status play, fourth wall, beats, actioning, split focus, arcs, journeys, flow were racing around the room. What was going on? I began to sweat.

The director pointed to a scene in my script and asked: "Whose reality is this?" My head nearly fell off.

In dramatic writing, people were using a whole slew of different techniques and concepts I hadn't heard of. Some were different words for familiar ideas, but many were entirely new to me.

They'd not only been using them for centuries. They'd been honing them before the most demanding audience of all – the living, breathing, impatient, hungry, fidgety and wonderful general public!

Call myself a writer? I'd hardly begun. I needed to sharpen up, and fast. I needed to get to grips with those techniques and tools. They were powerful. They were transformative. Some of them blew my mind.

So I looked for a book to set me right.

But there wasn't one.

No single book on the main dramatic techniques for writers new to that world.

So I had to work it all out on my own.

This was the start of a humbling, exciting, and powerful journey.

A journey into the world of dramatic writing, its craft and concepts. Thinkers and practitioners. Psychology, sociology and language. Stagecraft. Writing for people. Performers, characters and audience. What works in a room. Devouring films, TV and plays. Making notes. Dissecting. Trying things out. And above all, a practical, life-changing apprenticeship in the hands of experienced actors and directors.

I always wanted to be the best writer I could be, and earn access to that exciting world. It was far from easy.

I wrote this for my younger self, and for you, ambitious professional writers, so that you get there less painfully, and faster. Really for any writer who needs the helping hand I needed back then.

What This Book Can Do For You

If you're a **writer new to dramatic techniques**, the concepts in this book will blow your mind (as they did mine).

Imagine - a world of writing going on right under your nose, in action every time you watch TV, see a film, go to the theatre.

And you've no idea how it's done.

Sometimes, writers think scripts are just about writing great dialogue.

If that's you, hold onto your hat!

If you're an **ambitious writer looking for clear, powerful writing strategies**, this book will give you a treasure-chest.

You'll learn about shaping tension and time, using props to bring scenes alive, robust techniques for structure and editing.

You'll become bolder and more confident in shaping ideas.

You'll discover tools other writers still don't know about.

If you're an **experienced writer or writing teacher**, this book will inspire you in new directions.

You'll learn new skills to give your writing greater impact.

You'll sharpen your grasp of story, space and time.

You'll be more confident about developing ideas with editors, publishers and those you teach.

You'll also find an overview of

- ✵ influential thinkers and their main ideas
- ✵ further reading to take you deeper.

So! Are you ready to get started?

What's So Great About Dramatic Techniques?

Dramatic techniques are ancient. They've stood the test of time. They've been proven over hundreds of years. In front of live audiences ready to laugh, cry, or chuck tomatoes.

xviii

For centuries, dramatic writers have learned from live, unfiltered feedback - the ultimate market research. So, they've learned a trick or two.

Believe me, you can totally feel it when an audience doesn't get your eloquent speech, doesn't laugh at your hilarious joke, or switches off in boredom.

You feel every line that's out of whack. Every little self-indulgence.

You feel exactly when a word is too many, too few, or just right.

You feel it with your entire body.

That joke that jars a tiny bit in rehearsal – cut it. You put it in front of an audience, it's magnified a thousandfold. So, you become very clear about what needs to be cut or changed.

You don't want to leave it till the moment when you're in the theatre, amongst the audience, watching your play, and a complete stranger falls asleep by your side.

It was very hot, and he'd had an exhausting day. And it wasn't my play. It was a friend's. Yes, a friend's.

But with live audience feedback, there's nowhere to hide.

It's painful. And painful or not, you learn an amazing amount from it, and from other scriptwriters who put themselves through the same mill.

Over the centuries, this live trial by audience has distilled into a range of powerful dramatic techniques. It means drama insiders have a professional shorthand that helps them enormously in writing their scripts.

In the future, audiences will be wired up to machines, and other writers will learn what dramatists have always known.

In fact, it's already happening in film – with facial monitoring, biometrics, fMRI scans... It's called neuro-cinematics, and it's enough to put you off your popcorn!

But really, it's just a high-tech version of what experienced dramatists know from instinct.

And thankfully, technology will never completely fathom the unpredictable, shape-shifting live audience. Audiences are different, context is important, and even the time of day, current events and what they've just eaten or drunk can affect how a story goes down.

And if it were easy to write dramatically, everyone would do it brilliantly, and every play, film or TV show would be brilliant. Which isn't the case.

So, why make the effort to learn dramatic techniques? Because

- they're emotionally powerful
- they've been thoroughly audience-tested, sometimes over centuries
- they're bold and amplify your ideas
- they're clear and can travel
- they add a big extra string to your writing bow.

And here's the thing:

Dramatic techniques help you to step back from the close-up level of words. So, you can see the bigger picture of what you're writing.

Not just words, but story shapes and arcs. And not just shapes across a story, but also shapes across a scene, and shapes within it: objects, time, space, place, action, relationships between things, place and people, and how they all flow together.

They help you step beyond words, and orchestrate the multidimensional shapes and patterns of your writing.

They're that powerful.

How to Use This Book

I want this book to be practical and well used. I hope you'll scribble in it, fold the corners (or add highlights to the e-book) and add your own notes and discoveries.

If you don't like writing on books, get a hardback notebook for your viewing notes. The more you watch films, TV and plays in a mindful way, with notebook in hand, the more you'll learn for your own writing.

I suggest you skim-read the book once, to get a sense of what's in it.

Then cherry-pick the chapters that seem most useful for your writing. Do any exercises that jump out at you.

Finally, read each chapter slowly, and do the other exercises.

And importantly, after you do any writing, take time to reflect on what worked and didn't, and on what you've learned.

This reflective time often gets missed out, but it's vital. It's when your brain sees and consolidates learning. So it's very productive, and will turbo-charge your understanding and help it stick.

That's how courses work on the distance university education I teach.

And if you're the methodical type of writer, you can work through the book chronologically, as a self-study course.

You can also use it as a writing or teaching reference. Each section gives a suggestion of what to do next. There's also a recommended reading list for deeper insights into key topics.

Or maybe you're at an impasse, and looking for writing inspiration? If that's you, use the exercises as a lucky-dip or random stimuli, to help kick-start the next part of your scene or project.

So, let's get started. Happy writing! And don't forget to make notes in your writer's notebook.

PART I

Dramatic Foundations

The dramatic foundations up ahead are the cornerstones of dramatic writing.

Professionals in the performing arts know this stuff. It's a shared language. A shorthand that helps them to discuss work in progress effectively.

Writers with other writing backgrounds have often heard of these concepts. But typically, I've found that they don't use them in the same specific and practical ways.

Try thinking of writing as a body. Words are the clothes – what you see on the surface. They can be loud or quiet, patterned or pretty or revealing, well groomed or just thrown on, look-at-me shrieking neon, or minimalist low-impact grey. Words are the surface of your writing. They're what readers see and hear first.

Dramatic techniques, on the other hand, are the bones and muscles of the body. They're under the surface of the clothes. The framework that holds everything together.

To continue the analogy: you can have strong bones and muscles, or you can have a loose jumble in a rattling bag. A "large, loose baggy monster", if you like. That's how the novelist Henry James described poorly shaped novels. "Large loose baggy monsters" full of the "accidental and the arbitrary", where anything goes. And the phrase is so vivid that it has stuck as a warning of what not to do, if you want to write an engaging, compelling novel.

3

So where do bones and muscles fit with dramatic techniques? Well, they're what give stories shape, tension, momentum and impact.

When you watch a film or play, you feel its bones and muscles, through the emotional journey you experience. The emotional rollercoaster, if you like. With an emotional journey, you're not feeling the individual words, you're feeling the underlying shape. The journey, the ride.

It's a bit like when you listen to music, whether it's a big symphony with a grand finale or a subtle song with a hooky chorus.

You can feel an emotional journey on a big scale, through the overall story arc – for example, the way you feel at the climax of a powerful film.

Or you can feel it moment by moment, in the ebb and flow of tension and release.

Again, like listening to music: You can be swept up in the build and swell of a beautiful song. And you can be moved by individual phrases, riffs and chords.

When you're emotionally immersed in a journey like this, you're often hardly aware of individual words.

You're feeling those story bones and muscles.

Now, most writers want to get below the surface of words. They want to make an emotional connection with their readers.

But when you're writing and editing, you're close-up, wrangling individual words. The speed of writing words and the speed of experiencing story as a reader are very different. And it can be hard to detach enough to experience the story with fresh, new reader eyes.

So, it's really helpful for writers to have tools to help them wrangle their writing through a different frame. One that holds the writer away from the words.

This is where dramatic techniques really come into their own.

They provide building blocks at different scales and through different dimensions.

A bit like cogs in engineering. They can be tiny inside a watch, big inside a submarine or huge enough to support a bridge. Yet they still have the same shape and essence.

This next section starts with a zoom through two of drama's major building blocks: time and space. They're two of the key concepts in Aristotle's *Poetics*, which has had a huge influence on Western dramatic thinking.

These sections on time and space are followed by concepts for writing scenes, then other aspects of dramatic craft.

All the dramatic concepts are interdependent and feed into each other, just like cogs in a machine.

So you can read each section as a standalone. But they also act as lenses on each other, as alternative routes into the territory. For example, it's hard to talk about dramatic irony without talking about secrets, and vice versa. It's hard to talk about character wants and stakes without touching on fatal flaw and dramatic action.

So, each section will cross-refer you to others that are linked. Try following the threads to see where they lead. You'll eventually find everything links up into a cross-weave of interconnected dimensions.

Now, although this sounds a lot to take in, in practice, there are just a few key techniques that come up time after time. So get to grips with those, and you'll easily take your writing to a whole new level.

Let's dive first into the biggest concept of them all: Space.

Space

Learn powerful ways to visualize your story and its world.

The spatial concepts from film and stage are incredibly powerful for writers. Often, a space or place is the starting point for a story, or for a scene.

Imagine an empty space where anything can happen. Suddenly, a character arrives and a story magically starts.

Imagine a picture frame with a place inside it, ready to draw us right in and experience a story.

A space is a way into a world.

And the ways stories work spatially in film and stage have a lot to teach writers from other disciplines.

It's where I've had most to learn as a fiction writer moving into scripts.

Space is one of the three "dramatic unities" come down to us from Aristotle. He's the grandfather of dramatic theory, in a direct line to all the modern story gurus – Robert McKee, Syd Field, even Joseph Campbell, who wrote *The Hero's Journey*.

Aristotle's three dramatic unities of space, time and action are very useful tools for shaping story.

And space is a key ingredient of dramatic technique. A good handle on space and scenes will transform your writing.

The best way to understand scenes clearly is to use visualization techniques. You'll immediately be able to see their impact and potential, and edit far more confidently and productively.

So, let's get cracking!

Visualizing Space

Visualizations can really help writers to understand how to use space. When you write, you're trying to create pictures in the mind of your reader. But how do you know the crystal-clear image in your head is reaching your reader?

This clarity gap is the biggest problem I see in new writing. Writers think they're communicating clearly, because it's there in glorious technicolour, in their heads. But their words only cover a tiny fraction of what the reader needs to see. Or focus on the wrong things, in the wrong order, so the reader sees unrelated fragments and can't piece them together.

How can you create a clear picture for your reader, covering the right things, in the right order?

Film thinking can really help. Film is a visual medium. To take the audience on a journey, film makers use 'master shots', and weave them together. They have precise control over what we see, and when.

What's more, they understand how to use visual parameters to create precise emotional effects. They can influence whether we feel close-up intimacy, cool judgment, laughter, tears, or alienation.

The amazing filmmaker Charlie Chaplin said this: 'Life is a tragedy when seen in close-up, but a comedy in long-shot.' A tragedy in close-up, a comedy in long-shot.

Viewpoint affects emotional impact. Filmmakers understand this very clearly, and break it down and discuss it all the time. They have to use master shots, because they're collaborating with teams of people. So they get used to combining creativity with a systematic approach.

Writers also talk about viewpoint. They wrangle first person, third person, free indirect style, knowing and unreliable narrators. So there's some similarity with film. But fiction viewpoint is incredibly fluid. It can dart easily into the past, the future, dreams, thoughts, across the galaxy and inside an atom very easily. That freedom is wonderful, but it also comes with pitfalls. You can lose your reader on the way.

So for a storyteller, thinking about a film crew lugging a camera, setting it up, waiting for the right light and moment, can be really helpful.

That effort and cost means the director has to make very clear, effective choices.

So a director invests a lot of advance time studying emotional effects, storytelling craft, techniques. And they're techniques that can really benefit writers.

In my experience, fiction writers rarely think or study this way. They often outline the story, and maybe the scenes, but they rarely frame the shots, or the order of shots.

But there's a lot to learn from doing this, particularly by looking at storyboarding and cinematography. Cinematography is about the composition of shots – their look, appearance and what's in the frame. Storyboarding is the order of shots, and how your audience travels through the story. Every decision is calculated for clarity and emotional impact on the audience.

Now, this isn't about turning you into a scriptwriter. Film and cinematography are their own specialism. But even a basic knowledge can give you extremely useful tools for fiction. It can help you clarify your visual and spatial ideas. Make them bolder, with more powerful impact. And above all, control how your reader experiences the story.

And the great thing is, you can do this without paying a crew and lugging a camera around.

For example, maybe your chapter lacks focus. If so, you could try tighter framing. Get in closer to the characters. Maybe start with a wide-shot to establish context, and move in through a mid-shot to a close-up.

Or maybe you have a problem with head-hopping? A viewpoint that jumps in and out of heads, or sprayguns around the scene, looking at a clutter of details? Film shot framing can really help.

Or, maybe your characters feel unengaging? Could it be that your viewpoint is too detached? Maybe you have a far-off, god-like viewpoint but want your reader to connect with your characters? Again, film framing and understanding the impact of close-ups can help.

Or, maybe the pace is too slow? Film techniques apply to storytelling time as well as space. Time is covered in the next section. But time and space are inextricably linked. So start with space, and take it from there.

In short, film visualization techniques can help you structure your fiction storytelling for maximum impact. You'll be able to edit more quickly, effectively and confidently. And once you've mastered the techniques, you'll be able to write more quickly, too.

Here's an example from when I was working with a fiction writer. Let's call her Jan.

Like many new writers, Jan was trying to cram in far too much at the start of her novel. She had introduced a lot of descriptive detail, thinking this would help to bring the setting to life. But it was scattergun, jumping from one thing to the next. As a reader, I had to jump around mentally, and it was confusing. Despite all the detail, I still couldn't get properly oriented in the story.

But imagine the film equivalent. Your friend has a new video camera, and they're pointing it at everything in sight. From the sofa to the TV to through the window, into the garden, their child's smile, a door opening, and a closeup on the murder weapon lying bloodied on the floor.

Well, not in your friend's house, but you get the picture. It's like a spraygun. Instant vertigo! To the reader, leaping from detail to detail without a clear, controlled direction of travel, feels confusing. It feels unmoored, without an anchor, messy. The reader will switch off, though they may not be able to explain why. The film metaphor can help.

By thinking about film shots, Jan was able to organise a clear way in. An establishing shot on a suburban street, then into the house, sketch in some colour, and then in for a close-up on the murder weapon. Anything that distracted from a clear direction of travel could be cut, or moved into a better place in the sequence. The result? A clear, compelling opening that took the reader on a journey and painted the picture at the moment when it was needed.

So, as a way into visual thinking about space, let's now look at the different film master shots, and what impact they're used for. And don't worry about precise definitions here. Shot names are just a practical shorthand for the film industry. They're not set in stone, but they're extremely helpful for thinking about fiction setting, scene and viewpoint.

Wide shot (WS)

A large-scale view. Often a landscape or streetscape, taking in a large chunk of space.

Imagine a desert planet with two moons. Or a road with a beat-up car. Or a banquet table with loads of guests.

Wide shots cover a big space – anything from panoramic to the sweep of a room.

It's a fairly elastic kind of shot. But what's important is that a wide shot gives context for the characters. Because it gives the context, and the relationship between characters and their world, it's fantastic for heavy lifting. And it's great for story exposition – the backdrop to the story.

11

In film, wide shots are often used for orientation. You'll hear this called an "establishing" shot. It sets the scene. When you know the setting, and the relationship between the characters and their world, you immediately get a snapshot, a signpost, and a quick way into the story. It also has a particular emotional impact, which I'll go into shortly.

So a wide shot for context is tremendously helpful.

In fiction, the equivalent might be sketching in: a wide, dusty road, and two dark figures far way. Or a mediaeval hall with music and a banquet in full swing. Or a shop window full of glamorous ball gowns.

You immediately have an invitation into a world, and know the character context.   Surely, it goes without saying that these must be used all the time?

Well, no. Wide shots are great, but they have a particular emotional effect. A particular viewpoint. They feel emotionally detached.

And you may not want your audience, or reader, to feel emotionally detached from your characters.

With wide shots, you're placing the viewer far from the action, looking on. The effect is emotionally detached. A movie consisting entirely of wide shots would feel at a remove and epic, and the characters distanced, even ant-like. An example of this is the experimental film *Koyaanisqatsi: Life Out of Balance*. It shows distance shots of people, cityscape, landscape, clouds. The people are often speeded up and look like swarming bees. It has a hypnotic, repetitive soundtrack. The viewpoint is god-like. You're looking on, from a great distance. The viewpoint is the opposite of immersion and inclusion in that world.

Koyaanisqatsi is an extreme example. More typically, when wide shots are used, you get a wide shot followed by a closer-in shot of an interior, or characters.

For example, in the TV series *Friends*, you often see an outdoor wide shot of the apartment block, then it cuts to the interior of the apartment.

The journey from detached wide shot to a mid-shot brings you closer to the characters - literally and emotionally.

The effect on the reader is that you're being led into the story.

A wide establishing shot is often used as a visual shorthand. You don't need to close in gradually on a character. You can cut straight there. The viewer understands the convention.

The technique is so familiar to us that TV directors often create the context by using stock shots. Say, a Swiss mountain landscape, followed by a hut interior, shot in a movie studio. The audience easily makes the necessary imaginative leap.

You can place the shots the other way round, too: from close-up, out to wide shot, for a different emotional effect. One minute, you're close in with the romantic couple, lying on the grass. Then we pull away and see the surrounding countryside. Pulling away like this frames the character within a big landscape. Sometimes even a huge, epic landscape – the desert or the mountain top. This can create a sense of isolation, or a sense of grandeur, evoking the human spirit in a tough environment.

The fiction equivalents of wide shots, close-ups and other film shots can alert you to viewpoint issues. They help you, for example, notice dizzy zooming in, or contradictory direction of travel. This helps greatly with editing your writing for better flow.

TRY THIS:

The openings of scenes are crucial to engaging your reader with the story. I like to use the word "cogging", like the cogs of a wheel. Get your reader cogged with the story, then use clear flow and travel to keep the momentum going.

Try this out, by sketching a scene with a wide shot. Use words that give a sense of spaciousness and scale, the bigger picture. For example:

The sun was setting over the horizon...

Write a short sentence of your own that sketches in some scenery at this big scale. This will establish a clear perspective, and give us a clear entry point to the scene.

Then, trying homing in on the character. Still a wide shot, but a bit closer in:

> *Jem trudged along the drove road...*

Write your own next sentence at this closer scale.

Then try closer in still – a full shot, taking in Jem's whole body.

> *He pulled his coat tighter and his hat down hard against the chill wind.*

Note that visually, the effect is like a camera zooming in, from extreme wide shot to closer in. You're creating the illusion of visual travel, and transmitting it to your reader stage by stage.

How does it feel to your mind's eye?

TRY THIS:

Try experimenting with pace in your scene-setting. Now write a version of your opening where you flesh out the wide shot more. Give it a bit more detail.

> *The sun was setting over the horizon, turning the sky a lurid pink. The light was fading fast, and it would soon be hard to see the road. If it could be called a road...*

What does your new sentence feel like? Does it give a sense of space and bring the landscape to life? Or do you feel the need to cut to your character quicker? The answer will depend on the mood you want to create, and your genre. You might want

14

to settle the reader in gradually. Or you might want to sweep them off their feet for a fast-paced ride.

There's no right or wrong here. It's best to master different ways of playing with time, so that you have different techniques up your sleeve

If your pace doesn't vary, whether it's fast or slow, it'll quickly get boring for the reader.

You're aiming for a sweet spot between enough variety for interest, without overshooting into confusion.

Now, expand the second of your two "shots" – the closer-in, full shot, showing the general impression of your character. Develop what we see – maybe a general picture of what they're wearing, their silhouette or way of walking.

Do you feel your mind's eye staying with the general impression, or wanting to home right in, or darting about? Where do you feel the need to focus next?

When might you use this "closing in" approach? Think about how it might work in different genres.

TRY THIS:
Now, mix things up. Try some wide shots mixed with closer-in sentences, either extra detail at a close-up scale, or with a wildly diverging focus. For example:

> *The sun was setting over the horizon, and the*
> *moles were burrowing through the soil...*
> *Jem trudged along the drove road, as starlings*
> *roosted in the trees...*

These are extreme shifts in viewpoint! Try writing some extreme and some more subtle variations. What's the effect? How does your mind's eye respond to each?

What would the effect be, if this were filmed?

TRY THIS:
Now, write a sentence or paragraph with the wide and closer-in shots the opposite way around. That is, from close in, to extreme wide shot.

> *The sweat broke out on Jem's brow and trickled down under his collar. He trudged along the drove road as the sun dropped below the hill.*

What's the effect of this technique? How does it make you feel about the character? Where does it place you emotionally in relation to the character?
When might you use this technique?

Note: These viewpoint experiments aren't about turning your fiction into film writing.

The conventions of fiction are different to film. One of the wonderful characteristics of fiction is that it can travel fluidly in time and space, including mental space, and sweep the reader along.

But sometimes, writers push that fluidity too far, create confusion, and lose their readers. Using film shots can help you understand viewpoint and how it travels, and control the impact on your readers more effectively.

Full shot (FS)
A whole-body shot.

A full shot lets us see the character's whole body, from head to toe. It gives a general first impression.

The full shot was particularly popular in the early days of cinema. Early movies were often filmed in theatres, where you see the human scale. Audiences were used to taking in the whole person in real-life proportions.

Directors were still getting used to the intimacy of closer-in shots.

A full shot lets you see a character's body movements - their stride or shuffle, the swing of their arms, the hunch of their shoulders. It lets you see how they cover ground and take up space in a room. These movements give a sense of the character's personality, at a glance.

Full shots also show some of the context around the characters, so they can also give a sense of their social surroundings – their workplace, or where they live.

However, this viewpoint is more emotionally detached than a mid-shot or close-up. We're seeing the characters from a distance, beyond the range of human touch. Thinking of the other senses, we can hear them only when they shout, or talk loudly. We can't hear the detail of ordinary conversation, unless the surroundings are very quiet.

The full shot can be used as mid-way point after a wide shot, to bring us closer in to the character. Or, like the wide shot, it can be used as an establishing shot. Then, to get within natural earshot of the character, you'd probably want to close in further, to a mid shot.

TRY THIS:

Taking the wide shot sentence or paragraph you wrote, develop the character further, in a full shot. For example:

> *Jem trudged along the drove road, a hunched figure in a black coat and heavy boots.*

At this scale, think about gait, shape, how the character takes up space. What's the first impression, if you saw this person and didn't know them? Write that first. Then close in and give a little more detail, though still not a close-up. Perhaps their arms, their sense of purpose, what they're carrying, for example:

17

His hands were stuffed deep into his pockets
against the cold, and his scarf wrapped so thick
that his face couldn't be seen.

Where does your mind's eye want to go next?

TRY THIS:

In full shots, clothes are important. They give a crucial first impression. What stands out in your character? What's emblematic? Maybe a colour or item of clothing? Maybe their silhouette?

Fashion designers and fashion eras often have signature silhouettes - the A line, the New Look, the Vivienne Westwood bustle. Think about your character's silhouette. Are their clothes tight or loose? Short, or long and sweeping? Heavy and sculptural, or light and fluid, full of motion?

Try observing people in the street with your eyes half-closed. If they were characters, what would be the dominant impression?

Use your observations to write some full shot sentences.

TRY THIS:

Develop your sense of the full shot viewpoint more, by focusing on action. Again, what's the dominant impression? Are they agitated, purposeful, or still?

Where is your character heading? What's the direction of travel, or dramatic intention, of their movement? What verbs express that energy, intensity and purpose? Think about an actor conveying that character.

Does Jem stride, sashay, scuttle or thunder?

Now, write some new full shot material to insert into your paragraph.

Also try inserting a wide short element into the full section. What's the effect? Can you feel the difference in mental "travel" for the reader?

When might you use a full shot in your writing?

Mid shot or medium shot (MS)

A waist-to-head shot.

A mid shot is still closer in. It places us close to the characters, showing them essentially from the waist up. At this distance, we can see their interaction, and hear what they're saying. With this closer-in framing, we can probably hear their natural, public dialogue – everyday conversation. However, we might struggle to hear whispered or intimate dialogue.

On screen, a mid shot is by far the most used kind of shot. It's familiar because it's similar to the way we experience people we're talking to in a room. We're close enough to hear them and see them clearly. So in film, this kind of shot is strongly associated with realism and documentary.

The mid shot is a half-way house between full shot and close-up. It allows us to hear conversation, but doesn't have the intimacy of close-up.

With a mid shot, you can clearly see a character's face, hairstyle, colouring, expression. You'll also see more detail of their clothes - a sense of texture, and prominent patterns, for example. But you won't see the characters' bitten nails, Adam's apple or tiny stud earrings.

In movies and especially in interviews, mid shot is the dominant shot for dialogue between characters.

So, what about writing? Here's an example of midshot. Note, there's more detail and gesture, but not right up close:

> *Lara turned to him with a smile. "You took your time".*
> *She clipped the pen to her clipboard, and nodded toward the shiny glass door.*

For comparison, here's Jem in full shot.

> *Jem trudged along the drove road, a hunched figure in a black coat and heavy boots.*

19

And Lara in mid shot again:

> *Lara turned to him with a smile. "You took your*
> *time".*
> *She clipped the pen to her clipboard, and nodded*
> *toward the shiny glass door.*

Through the writing, you're showing the reader what they can see. If they can see a pen, they're in pretty close. If they're seeing a hunched figure on a drove road, they're pretty far away. And you have complete control over what you invite them to see.

Of course, the film shots aren't that cut and dried, and the human imagination certainly isn't. So writing can be far more fluid. You can take the reader with you.

There are countless creative possibilities and combinations.

Filmmakers often play around with the scale of visuals, and the sound might be in a different viewpoint to the visual. For example, you often see a panoramic wide shot of characters walking far off in the landscape, while we hear their close-up voices. It doesn't have to be realistic.

But being aware of shots will help you make informed decisions about flow, scale, what's natural and what's experimental. Then you can make the appropriate choice for your genre and story.

TRY THIS:

Develop your previous paragraph by writing a mid shot. With this framing, think of the characters' stance, what they're wearing, facial expression and hairstyle. What are they doing? Are they static, or in motion? Can you see their intention from their physical action?

Develop this mid shot into a full paragraph. Now, play around with mixing different shots into the mid shot – wide shot, full shot and close-up. What's the effect?

As you arrange your shots, notice the visual "travel" - the spatial journey through the different shots in your mind's eye. Does it flow smoothly? Does anything jar? What's your preference? When might you choose each variation?

Close up (CU) and extreme close up (ECU)

Anything from a head-and-shoulder shot to someone's fingernails.

A close up covers a wide range of different scales, from the natural close-up of close human contact to the heightened extreme close-up of very close or even microscopic proximity.

At close-up scale, you can see someone's teeth, wrinkles, the tilt of their head, and hear them murmur. At extreme close-up, you can see their chipped nail polish, shirt stains and tremors, and hear their breathing.

The key expressive quality of close-up is intimacy. Close-up and extreme close-up shots give us privileged insight. This can have different emotional effects, depending on the context.

For example, if the characters are familiar to us, a close-up draws us closer, inviting us to deepen our bond. But if they're unfamiliar, a close up can feel intrusive and even alienating. In some contexts, too, extreme close-ups can be used for comedic effect, as in looking up someone's nose, or focusing on the hole in their sock.

Close-ups are on a spectrum from naturalistic to unnatural, depending on how far they depart from normal human vision.

If you're into photography, it might be helpful to think of the different lenses: a 50mm lens mimics typical human vision, so it's used for full shot, and mid shot. A 17-40mm zoom is used for wide angle or wide shot. A lens upward of 50mm is used for macro shots – close-up, or extreme close-up.

A macro lens is often used to reveal mysteries and textures that are hidden from the everyday human gaze. *A drop of dew on a blade of grass. The wings of a moth.*

So how might this work in writing?

Fiction can easily zoom right into an extreme close-up. Tiny sensory details can create a sense of extraordinary intimacy and vividness.

> *The dark red blemish on his cheek... the torn edge of her pocket... the yellow specks of paint on the carpet...*

These details put readers right up, nose to nose, with what the writer is describing.

Note that you don't have to say anything about the distance. You don't need overt signposts – for example, prepositions such as *near* or *close to*, or verbs such as *peered* or *squinted at*.

To bring your readers this close, all you need to do is choose and frame exactly what your readers see.

> *The dark red blemish on his cheek... the torn edge of her pocket... the yellow specks of paint on the carpet...*

TRY THIS:

Develop your paragraphs in progress by writing some close up and extreme close up detail. As you do this, think about not just the visual elements. Think of all the different senses, and what each brings.

At extreme close-up, touch, texture and smell become even more important.

Brainstorm texture and smell words for the situation you're describing. Do they work differently at this different scale?

TRY THIS:

Close-up and extreme close-up don't just apply to description. They also apply to actions.

However, action words can change at these different scales. Readers are close enough to notice different nuances.

So, brainstorm verbs for the close-up viewpoint in your paragraph.

> *His fingers shook as he opened the tin. Her hand grazed the torn edge of her pocket. He flicked a speck of ash onto the carpet.*

Compare them with the verbs for your full and wide shots. Do they have different sound qualities?

> *Stride, thunder, sashay.*
> *Shook, grazed, flicked.*

TRY THIS:
Write some extreme close-up description into your work in progress, and explore the effect. How does extreme close-up change how the reader is positioned emotionally towards the character? How easy is it to follow the "travel" in your mind's eye?

Brainstorm some narrative situations where you might want to use extreme close-up. Why might you choose this viewpoint? Does genre play a role?

When and why might you choose to avoid extreme close-up?

TRY THIS:
Choose a passage from your previous writing, or writing by someone whose work you admire. Use a highlighter pen to mark up descriptive language that suggests a particular type of shot.

How does the writer show how the reader is positioned, literally and emotionally?

Are we literally far away and detached, or close up and personal?

If you wanted to alter the focal length to bring the reader closer, or distance them more, which elements would you need to change?

Compare your own writing with a favourite published author's. What do you notice?
How might this thinking help your editing process?

Mental Spaces

Fiction is fantastic for getting inside characters' heads. Whereas dramatic writing, as discussed, is more about externalising, and revealing inner lives through action. Script action must be played, so there are more limitations. Whereas fiction viewpoint can swoop around with enormous freedom.

You can go right inside characters' heads, and report their thinking directly.

> *"What a fabulous idea!" she thought.*

Or use free indirect style for a more oblique way into the character's head.

> *She nodded. It was a fabulous idea. Trust Jade to come up with it!*

And fiction has mind-blowing potential to dart around in time, space, and different characters' heads, as in:

> *He slapped his forehead. Wow. That was unexpected. She'd never told him she could speak Spanish.*

25

This extraordinary fluidity and freedom of fiction can be a problem for some writers.

In your head, you know exactly what you're on about. Everything's entirely clear in your wild, freewheeling mind. But readers can't read your mind. They can only read your words.

So, they may be confused because their brain and background aren't exactly the same as yours. I see a lot of fiction in progress which suffers from this problem.

Drama, by its nature, has to be more rigorous with mental travel and geography, and has useful ways of thinking about this.

So, dramatic thinking can be a real help to authors whose writing needs greater clarity.

Here's a look at some ways that drama handles mental spaces, and how to use them.

And by the way, the film director Alexander Mackendrick coined the wonderful phrase "invisible imaginary ubiquitous winged witness". He describes the movie camera viewpoint as a "winged witness" which can fly around and spy on characters. It's invisible, and it can go everywhere, close up, far away and yes, even inside people's heads. "Invisible, imaginary, ubiquitous winged witness." Maybe in some ways, the camera and fiction viewpoints aren't that different after all.

Dramatic monologue

Hamlet: To be, or not to be. (Or: Should I kill myself?)

The dramatic monologue and its close cousin, the soliloquy, are first person narratives. They're from the "I" viewpoint, or the "we" viewpoint.

So clearly, they're a good way to get right inside a character's mental space.

Fiction writers and poets are used to writing in first person. They're aware of the pros and cons – the closer-intimacy,

26

the narrower focus, issues of exposition and voice, unreliable narrators. And by and large, they know how to make the best of these qualities in their writing.

So, what's new? Why are first person storytelling and dramatic monologue different?

The key is the word "dramatic".

Making your first-person stories dramatic will make them more compelling. And as you know, dramatic has a specific meaning that's really helpful for writers.

So, first, what's a dramatic monologue, and what's a soliloquy?

With a monologue, there's a listener, and the character knows this. They're speaking to that implied listener. By contrast, a soliloquy is the character's private thoughts, and we're eavesdropping.

Probably the most famous soliloquy in theatre is William Shakespeare's "to be or not to be", spoken by Hamlet. Hamlet is speaking to himself, and the audience can overhear his inner thoughts. He's wrestling with a dilemma: "To be, or not to be." Should he kill himself? What are the pros and cons?

For a famous monologue, check out the *Talking Heads* series by British playwright Alan Bennett. They're much loved and performed by amateur groups. They've been rerecorded for the BBC with a new generation of actors, including *Killing Eve's* Jodie Comer and Martin Freeman of *The Hobbit* fame.

The key point is that a dramatic monologue has a target.

Meet the imaginary listener

A dramatic monologue has a target. The characters are speaking to a listener. Who? Maybe to someone the character knows. Or someone they want to listen. A kind of confidante.

So, how can you use this in your writing?

Well, with a dramatic monologue, the actor needs to decide the target. Who they're speaking to. The addressee can't be just floating around, unmoored.

A monologue needs to be projected to someone. They won't usually be named, but they'll be imagined in the actor's head.

Maybe it's the character's boss or spouse. Or their community at large. Their dog. Or an imaginary confidante: their alter ego, or their better self. Maybe their unborn child or dead lover. Or they're speaking to anyone out in space listening when they're floating around in a capsule with no fuel. I've even written a monologue addressed to a theatre building, personified as a character.

A monologue addressed to a target, an imagined confidante, has clearer energy.

Even if the target isn't present or named, there's a built-in focus, and a sense of two-way interaction.

Hamlet's soliloquy is dramatic, because he's debating, interacting with an imagined confidante. The confidante might be himself – a kind of self-talk – or it might be the world at large. Either way, the soliloquy has interactive, two-way energy, and we in the audience feel that charge.

Sitting in the theatre, we're standing in for the imaginary confidante. We become the target. Which makes the storytelling far more engaging.

So, to strengthen your first-person writing, deciding the target is a useful decision you can make to create dramatic energy. Who's the story addressed *to*? Who is the narrator speaking to?

Note that you don't need to name the target overtly. They can just be implied. In fact, you may want to keep this information back, as it can be a powerful reveal for later. As an example of this, and spoiler alert: *We Need to Talk About Kevin* by Lionel Shriver is a classic of this technique.

Friend or foe?

In radio, new presenters are often advised: "Imagine you're speaking to a friend." Someone you feel at ease with, and can project towards with confident, relaxed energy.

They presenter doesn't say "Hey, Jack! Hey, friend!" when they're speaking on air. Just by implying the imaginary friend, they create powerful two-way energy.

But in fiction, the target or confidante doesn't need to be a friend. They don't need to be on the narrator's side.

In fact, they could just as easily be the opposite. Someone the narrator doesn't trust. Or someone judgemental they want to convince.

A narrator might have a variety of reasons for speaking. For example, they might want to justify themselves, or cover their tracks. Plead for forgiveness. Leave a legacy for their unborn baby. Warn or persuade their tribe.

Their reason for telling the story can also change over its course. There might be a sense of mental "travel", or a journey.

For example, maybe the narrator starts out angry and defensive, trying to cover their tracks. And over time, through telling their story, they realise what they need is forgiveness or redemption from their community. Again, you don't need to state this overtly. But it might colour the narrator's tone of voice, and give a sense of a long emotional arc.

Say, for example, the narrator is a police officer. The implied target is the wife of their dead work buddy. But gradually, the focus shifts to the community as a whole.

Note: when you first start writing, you might not know the narrator's reason for telling this story. That's OK. It might emerge while you're writing. Then you can go back and tweak that energy, on a later editing pass.

Knowing the reason for speaking, and the addressee, can give your story an extra dramatic and narrative layer. It'll help you write with a clearer intention and focus, as well as an overall dynamic.

And don't forget that the narrator's reason for telling the story might be to entertain.

TRY THIS:

Choose a piece of first-person writing in progress, and decide who the narrator is speaking to – the confidante, or target. Thinking of the radio technique of addressing an imaginary friend, sketch in this person as a specific character.

Are they a friend? A brother? A colleague? How old are they? What's their status, relative to the narrator? More power, less power? Wealthier, less wealthy? More optimistic, more pessimistic? Do they have more freedom, or less?

Then, explore the narrator's reason for telling their story to this character? The dramatic action. Is it to warn, inspire, persuade, entertain, inform? Can you identify a dramatic action for the whole story?

Try exploring two very different targets, and rewrite the passage in two ways. Does this affect the word choice and energy?

Mental geography

You can choose an imaginary listener for a whole novel, to create an overall projection focus.

But you can also look at a character's mental projection or mental map within a scene.

Take Hamlet's immortal line:

To be or not to be.

At one level, the character is projecting out into the room and towards the audience. So, there are practical, physical considerations about the target, and speaking loudly enough for the audience to hear.

But there's also mental projection – where the actor locates the target in his head. Even though it looks like straight first-person, there are lots of possible mental maps. And Hamlet doesn't use "I". He uses "we". So, he's implicitly widening the focus beyond himself.

Some of the possibilities are:

- Is Hamlet talking to the theatre audience, asking for advice?
- Is he talking to himself, and we're overhearing his self-talk?
- Is he thinking to himself, and we're hearing what's inside his head?
- Is he pretending to talk to himself, but aware he might be overhead by the courtiers (playing "mad")?

And even beyond that, what are we, the audience, in Hamlet's mental map?

- Do we exist in the character's reality, and he's addressing us directly as fellow sufferers in the world?
- Do we exist in the world of the play, and we're standing in for eavesdropping courtiers?
- Do we exist only in his head, and we're his inner demons?
- How much "knowing" or complicity is there between the performer and the audience? Are we invisible to Hamlet, or is there a fourth wall breach?

It's complicated! And it's one of the reasons Hamlet's soliloquy is so rich and challenging for actors.

But these are basic framing decisions an actor must make, to give the monologue a focus.

Without that, it's hovering unmoored in space. It has no clear target.

The ambiguity might pass by unnoticed in fiction and writing, which is more fluid in its use of mental space. But if your writing needs a clearer focus, it's worth considering some of these questions.

31

TRY THIS:
Watch some film versions of the "nunnery" scene from *Hamlet*. Search for "Hamlet nunnery scene" under "videos". You'll find lots of clips online, including ones with Mel Gibson, Jude Law and David Tennant.

It's a scene between Hamlet and his girlfriend, Ophelia. In this scene, Ophelia has been sent to speak to Hamlet. She knows her father is listening in the wings. Hamlet thinks they're being overheard. This affects the target of the speech. Sometimes, he's talking directly to Ophelia. Sometimes, he's talking so the eavesdroppers can hear.

In each clip, first note the physical space. Is the actor in a large, exposed space, or a narrow, intimate one? How does this change the actor's physical projection?

Then, think about the eavesdroppers. How close are they? Does Hamlet know he's being overheard? Notice how knowing shifts the target of the speech.

Then, note any shifts in the target. When is the speech between the couple, when is it out towards the eavesdroppers? Is Hamlet sometimes speaking to himself? Are there clear beats or moments where the target changes?

This awareness of targeting and mental placement can help you with tighter editing.

You can use it to frame your narrative more clearly, or to play games with your reader, as Hamlet does.

The nature of the target makes a big difference to how characters behave. This will come up later in when I discuss Goffman, *The Presentation of Self in Everyday Life*.

Bold framing and reframing of the target is used to devastating effect in the novels *We Need to Talk About Kevin* by Lionel Shriver, and Ian McEwan's *Atonement*. I won't spoil them for you by explaining how – you'll have to read them!

Cognitive maps and metaphors

A cognitive or mental map is someone's worldview - their way of seeing the world. In a way, it's like a supercharged version of a metaphor.

This is different to transient metaphors you might use in a sentence or paragraph. For example, "my love is like a red, red rose".

A cognitive map is more about someone's overarching frame on the world.

On the one hand, this might be because they have a particular job or interest. They might be sporty, and use lots of sports language:

> *You're onto a winner.*
> *He's a team player.*
> *That was a home run.*

Or they might be drawn to the natural world, and use animal or environmental metaphors:

> *Lower in the pecking order.*
> *We'll just have to wing it.*
> *That'll separate the wheat from the chaff.*

This is a good way to help develop a character's voice. For example, you could brainstorm words from the world they're in, and use them to inflect the character's speech.

But cognitive maps aren't just about big thematic metaphors, such as sport, nature, money, health, or war.

They're also about smaller linguistic markers that say a lot about us. For example, simple features, such as how we use the word "I" or "but".

Studying language is a good way to reveal someone's mental maps. For example:

33

What pronouns does your character use? A lot of first person "I" or "we"? Or second person "you"? Or neither? These are very different characters, with different kinds of interpersonal focus.

Is their language full of modal verbs (*might, should, can't*)? Maybe they're prone to hedging and uncertainty.

Do they use a lot of abstraction (*peace, terror, stuff*)? Or do they talk about specific details, such as texture, nuanced colours, sounds, smells?

What's their sensory bias? Is their dominant sensory mode visual, aural, or tactile? Do they say I hear you or I see what you mean?

Are their dominant metaphors strongly physical and intense, as in: "hit it, kick ass, hammer home"?

Or gentler, as in: "whisper it, paper over the cracks, sow a seed"?

Mental maps aren't just in colourful images. They can just as easily be hidden in someone's spatial words, including ordinary prepositions and verbs. For example, a character who says "going places, go for it, out there" might have big horizons.

One who says "on it, here and now, into it" might have a spatial focus closer to home.

Language and text analysis reveal a great deal about people's thought patterns and preferences. You can use this to help create characters that are more distinct from each other, more consistent and nuanced. It can also help you to get away from your own limiting language grooves and patterns.

Experts in linguistics study the fine nuances of language like this, and show how everyday language is full of hidden assumptions.

If you're interested in this territory – and it's fascinating – check out *I Is An Other: The Secret Life of Metaphor and How it Shapes the Way We See the World* by James Geary.

TRY THIS:
Choose a job title, such as a butcher, baker, or web designer. Now imagine that person in love. What metaphors would they use to describe their passion?

William Shakespeare used metaphors from nature, as in *Shall I compare thee to a summer's day?*

The Scottish scientist-poet James Clerk Maxwell wrote a *Valentine from a Telegraph Clerk* to another clerk, telling her he was "charged to a volt with love for thee".

What might a baker say in a love poem? Might they talk about perfect crusts and crumbs? Or the heat of the oven?

Write a passage using your chosen job metaphor.

TRY THIS:

Find out more about your own cognitive map by pasting a sample of your writing into one of the online sites that use linguistic analysis.

Here's an article on my site that links to Wordle: https://www.method-writing.com/writing-tips-shakespeare-lancaster-university-language-detectives/

Here's another tool that reveals verbs and nouns, and some insights about why this is useful:

https://www.method-writing.com/secret-life-verbs-nouns-writing-visualization-tool/

The site 750 Words also gives simplified view of the emotional focus of your writing. You need to join up, then you can paste in your text for analysis. https://750words.com/

Asides

The aside is another way of showing the speaker's inner life, this time with the audience as a knowing conspirator.

An aside is a short comment where the actor speaks directly to the audience, and the other characters don't hear. For example, the evil Iago in Shakespeare's Othello tells the audience:

> *Iago: I'll trap him with my tricks.*

35

He tells us his inner thoughts directly, straight towards us in the audience. The other characters are oblivious.

This is different to a monologue. It's a moment of conspiracy. We, the audience, are in on the secret. We're treated like privileged friends.

This technique is like extending a hand straight to the audience. It breaches the invisible fourth wall between actors and audience.

Asides are often used in comedy, to create a conspiratorial connection with the audience, and increase tension and "knowingness". Examples from screenwriting include the movies of Woody Allen, and the TV comedy *Malcolm in the Middle*.

Asides are also used in thrillers and dramas, usually as a way to enjoy the sinister inner life of the villain. Notable examples include Shakespeare's *Othello*, and the TV series *House of Cards*.

An aside has an inbuilt paradox. It's both intimate and alienating. It can create trust and distrust, at the same time.

Overall, an aside is a move away from realism, towards a heightened, more theatrical approach. It's a fun technique to explore and add to your box of writing tools. In fiction, it can be called an example of "metafiction" – a fiction technique which draws attention to the artifice of the story.

TRY THIS:
Taking a section of your writing in progress, try adding some asides. Make the narrator speak out directly to the reader.

What's the effect on the relationship between reader and narrator? Think about distance, status, intensity, flow, narrator trust, and register.

Next, try some variants with the direct address "you", and with different registers. What's the effect on the relationship?

How might you use this understanding to create more or less connection to your reader?

Adverbs

With an aside, the narrator is breaching the fourth wall, giving their direct opinion.

But there's another, subtler way for the narrator to breach the fourth wall: the adverb.

This might come as a surprise! Adverbs are incredibly common words. We use them all the time, without thinking.

But in fiction, they betray the presence of the narrator. They're an extra layer of comment, in the author's voice.

Consider this example:

> *It was a dark and stormy night.*

Now this:

> *It was a dark and horrendously stormy night.*

The night wasn't just dark and stormy. The narrator has an opinion about it. Horrendous! They're probably battening down the windows and shivering in a corner as we speak.

Compare:

> *It was a dark and thrillingly stormy night.*

Only one word has changed, but it's now a very different narrator. This one is probably a character from *Wuthering Heights*, out on the moors, enjoying the full elemental force of nature.

Of course, not all adverbs are this emotionally loaded. Some are very non-committal. Or *pretty, rather, more or less* non-committal:

> *It was a dark and very stormy night.*
> *It was a dark and quite stormy night.*

But they still reveal the narrator and their feelings about the night. Being "not that bothered" is still a viewpoint. Maybe they're completely used to dark, stormy nights, or being dryly understated while Hurricane Hannibal is raging outside.

Simple or not, adverbs always make the narrator visible, and so create an additional narrative frame.

That's one of the reasons why fiction writers are often advised to avoid adverbs.

Naturally, all words imply a viewpoint. Vocabulary choices, register, pronouns, and conjunctions all combine to create an inescapable editorial lens.

But adverbs have a strong viewpoint, and are particularly easy to spot.

TRY THIS:

Use the sentence "it was a dark and stormy night", or another simple sentence of your choosing. Experiment with adding adverbs.

Firstly, brainstorm different adverbs within the sentence, and make notes about the kind of characters evoked.

Then, imagine people you know. Brainstorm the adverbs they might use in your sentence, in different emotional circumstances. For example, fear, relief, rage, self-deprecation.

What do you discover about the impact of adverbs?

TRY THIS:

Now, choose a passage of text with a third person viewpoint. Highlight all the adverbs. What's their effect? What do you gain or lose by removing them?

Plot the adverbs on a line, ranging in intensity from forceful, high impact and colourful, to bland or vague.

Now, play around with each adverb within the sentences. Swap them around and see the effect.

Next, get rid of all adverbs. Read aloud the versions and compare them.

Do you need the adverbs? Can you put some of their force into stronger verbs?

How might you use this understanding in your writing and editing?

Frame narrators

Some dramas have a frame narrator who serves as the viewpoint character for the story.

A character who speaks an aside typically pops up from time to time. A frame narrator typically appears as a "bookend" at the start and end of the script, as well as in between. So, it's a sustained narrative device.

The effect is like a picture frame, making us aware of a degree of artifice. We're given a clear signal that we're about to witness a story contained within a story.

Stage examples include the Stage Manager in *Our Town* by Thornton Wilder, Tom in *The Glass Menagerie* by Tennessee Williams, and Puck in Shakespeare's *A Midsummer Night's Dream*. Movie examples include *Out of Africa*, with its voiceover narration, or *Annie Hall*, with Woody Allen's direct-to-camera address.

Frame narrators can also appear throughout the story, to add commentary, and keep the detaching frame alive in the audience's mind.

A frame narrator in drama is still a character in their own right, and not just a narrative device. They need to be fully realised as people.

It's easier to fudge this in fiction. The narrator can be elusive and shapeshifting, and you may prefer this ambiguity, or the detachment of a neutral third person viewpoint. But you may want to bring the narrator to life as a fully realised character.

Thinking about a frame narrator being physically embodied, as they are in drama, will help you explore the personality of your narrator with more clarity.

If you do this, you might want to consider parameters such as different degrees of intimacy, status, power, knowledge of the audience and the other characters in the story.

Is the narrator in the story, or on the outside, looking on?

Other parameters to explore include register and interactivity. A frame narrator who says: "Hey, listen up, folks!" is a different character to one who says: "Once upon a time..."

TRY THIS:

Taking an excerpt from your writing in progress, add an opening and closing narrator frame. What's the effect on the reader? How does it make you think and feel about the enclosed story?

Try several variations, exploring the qualities of intimacy, status, and involvement in the story. How does each affect the impact of your story?

Explore who your frame narrator is as a character. Are they involved in the core story, a player within it, or separate, looking on? What happens if you change this parameter?

How is your narrator positioned in relation to the time and location of the core story? How many days or years have passed? Is this important? What's the effect?

A story-within-a-story frame is often used in supernatural stories, as a playful way of priming the audience, or settling them in.

Explore other reasons why a narrator might tell a story in this way. Who are they speaking to? Single or plural audience? Public or private setting?

What's their drive behind the story? Entertainment, witness, reflection, redemption? How does this affect the impact of the story?

Playful & poetic

Typically, drama deals with a group of characters, and multiple external viewpoints. But dramas can also show a single viewpoint: the inner life inside someone's head. Scripts like this can make great use of drama's capacity to show and physicalise interior action.

For example, Alan Ayckbourn's *Woman in Mind* takes us inside the head of Susan, who is suffering from mental health problems. It shows us scenes from her mundane real life, as well as her perfect imaginary life, with a fantasy husband, son, and daughter. Her fragile mental state is shown through the use of apparent gibberish ("December bee" for "remember me"). The action moves seamlessly between her inner and outer worlds.

In the stage play *Realism* by Anthony Neilson, the entire play takes play in the main character's head. Everything shown on stage is a figment of his imagination, and hilariously surreal. The frame ending shows the boring reality of his actual life.

The plays of Sarah Kane are a tour de force in representing mental complexity. They're laid out like poetry, with a fragmented style, and fluid scene transitions and characters.

Movies with a mental health theme include *A Beautiful Mind* and *Inside Out*. Like the other scripts, they show bold ways of dramatizing someone's inner life. And they do it not by showing actions that reveal internal emotions. Rather, they embody the characters' interior lives. It's as though the characters have been turned inside out. Which is far more interesting than someone talking about their feelings.

TRY THIS:
See if you have any moments in your writing where characters are talking about their feelings.

Explore ways of dramatizing this. Brainstorm possible dramatic actions. Go deeper than, for example, throwing things around to express anger, or sitting down and sighing with a cup of tea, to express relief.

Dig deep into the interaction between characters, and between public and private self. This will help you to create more subtext and interest.

For example, an angry character unable to show it because they're in a high-level meeting might be scribbling the vilest graffiti onto their notepad.

Or, a relieved character who loosens their belt and kicks off their painful heels might find someone they want to impress walking in at their most embarrassing moment.

Find ways to represent both inner and outer life in the same scene.

TRY THIS:

Explore different ways of expressing mental states through language.

People who feel highly emotional don't usually speak coherently. Extreme joy or excitement might drive them towards over-the-top language. Extreme agitation or nerves might make them speak in confused fragments.

Nervous people might also self-reassure by talking to themselves. Or to imagined others, or objects around them, and then laugh at their own ridiculousness. How can you dramatize their feelings and mental journeys in your writing?

Look at sections where the character's mental state is under pressure, and shake up their language.

See also: Fourth Wall, Dramatic Irony, Epic, Transformation, Goffman.

Further reading:
Donnellan, D. (2013) *The Actor and the Target*. Nick Hern Books, London.

Time

In dramatic technique, time has its own distinctive ways of operating.

In fiction and poetry, readers can travel through time in a very fluid way. Mental backflips, exposition and asides can all be tucked in very easily.

Whereas in dramatic writing, time tends to be "chunked". The basic unit of drama is, after all, the scene - a discrete chunk of time and space.

And time can be chunked even smaller into moments and beats.

Unless you've studied scriptwriting, you probably won't notice this at all. Watching a screen story is a pretty seamless experience.

But you're probably intuitively familiar with the playful ways that films can arrange chunks of time and space, including flashbacks, montage, fades and cuts.

These techniques are relatively new in storytelling, and were revolutionary in their day. During the early days of film, most movies were filmed like stage productions, with long takes and a single camera angle. But very quickly, movie makers discovered new techniques such as scene cuts, close-ups and montage.

They also discovered how to speed up time and slow it down.

For fiction writers and poets, it's useful to look at the different ways drama can handle time. It'll help to broaden your creative vocabulary, and give you more clarity about when and how to use the different choices.

43

But first, let's go back to early Greek drama and Aristotle's *Poetics*, when time was first mentioned as a cornerstone of dramatic technique.

The dramatic unity of time

The "dramatic unities" comes down to us from Aristotle's *Poetics*. It refers to a kind of story sent in a single day, in a single setting, with a single dramatic action. So unities of time, place and action.

A classic play that embodies the unities of time, place and action is Sophocles' *Oedipus Rex*.

It's a tragedy about Oedipus, a man who murders his father and sleeps with his mother, without knowing it's her. It starts in the morning, and ends in the evening of the same day. It takes place in a single location: the royal palace in the city of Thebes. And the story has a single action: Oedipus' quest to find out who murdered his father. And the murderer turns out to be him.

It's a wonderfully tight and tangled thriller plot, and a lot of the tension comes from the pressure cooker effect of the three unities: time, place and action.

But Aristotle wasn't writing a manual on playwriting. The three dramatic unities were simply a description of a technique he thought worked well on stage.

Many playwrights since then, including Shakespeare, haven't bothered about the dramatic unities at all.

But the dramatic unities have been highly influential in dramatic thinking. Why?

Firstly, limiting the time frame helps to increase tension.

Thinking of a pressure cooker, if you heat things up in a confined space, it'll get hotter, faster. A tight time frame, such as a week or single day, will make the action more heightened and exciting. It will feel more energetic, because you're packing more in.

Whereas without a tight time frame, the energy of a story can be dissipated.

44

For example, say your heroes are speeding through a city in their car, hot on the heels of the villains. The villains zoom up a side street and escape. The chase is called off for the night. The heroes have a shower, a decent sleep and a hearty breakfast. Then, in the morning, they head out for stage two of their hunt to the death.

Doesn't sound that thrilling, does it?

The whole energy and urgency of their mission has evaporated.

A tight time frame and tension are linked to the force of a character's "want" or motivation. If your protagonist really, really wants something, urgently, they won't hang about. They'll get out there and take immediate action.

So look closely at your scenes and their dramatic actions, and see whether they can be compressed in time.

I find it helpful to think of a picture frame, and how it might be placed around a story. Over a day, a morning, a month? Can any of the actions be combined in a scene, to raise the stakes?

How can you frame and arrange the story points for maximum impact?

For example, say it's Monday, and your protagonist finds out that her partner is a mass murderer. Don't let her wait till Tuesday to tackle him about it.

Instead, frame the scene so that the two actions are compressed. It can be helpful to think: get in late, get out early. You could start the scene at a point where the discovery has already happened. Maybe she's lived with the knowledge for a day, building up her torment, but hasn't had a chance to tackle him yet. And he's about to arrive at the door.

This framing will prime the scene with a powerful tension and subtext. Maybe at the start of the scene, your protagonist keeps the lid on her anguish. She wants to know more. Give him the benefit of the doubt. But pressure builds. She's behaving more and more oddly. Until finally, she blurts out what's brewing inside.

Time compression can be much more powerful than spinning out the action into two separate scenes. And here's another tip for super-charging your story.

A day like no other

The day a story happens isn't an ordinary day. It's a day like no other. It's a highly significant, charged day when the world is turned upside down.

It's a day when the status quo is disrupted, and everything changes.

It's a day when the protagonist is suddenly up against it, and takes decisive, momentous action.

If it isn't an unusual kind of day, why write a story about it?

So, a useful question when framing your story in time is: "Why today, of all days?"

What's so special about this day that the story urgently needs to kick off now?

Then, rearrange story events to emphasize this day.

For example, if it's about a school prom going drastically wrong, don't start it the month before, when preparations are getting underway. Start it on the morning of the prom, when the students already have their partners, outfits and arrangements set up. Leave them no time to wriggle out of their problems. Then they'll be really up against it – in the pressure cooker!

Make the time frame for your story as small as possible, getting in late and getting out early. And do the same for your scenes.

As a storyteller, you're in charge of time. It's one of your main tools for shaping your audience's experience. So, it's fine to be bold and robust in your approach.

If an event has a more drastic impact on the eve of the wedding, rather than the week before, put it there.

Your job isn't to make life easy for your characters. Quite the contrary! Your job is to give them a hard time, and see what they're made of.

Timeframe is one way you can put characters under serious pressure, and extract more dramatic juice from the situation they're in.

Ticking clocks

Movie fans are familiar with the "ticking clock" trope. The bomb countdown, the egg timer running out of sand.

A ticking clock device is simply any kind of deadline that puts characters under pressure.

If you set up a deadline, this compresses time and ups the ante.

Ticking clocks come in different varieties. They can be about time, of course. For example, a bomb counting down in the hold of the spaceship, a train about to leave for Paris, a wedding ceremony and the "I do" moment.

Or, they can be other cut-off points which raise the stakes. For example, someone's medication running out, the death of a crucial witness, two characters crossing paths, the hero's fingers clinging to a crumbling cliff.

In all these situations, the cut-off dynamic compresses the action, and builds excitement.

It needn't be something really obvious, or a big gesture. It can be something simple: running out of firewood, the sun going down, a car on its last legs. Anything that builds the pressure on your characters, and forces them closer to a decision point.

So if one of your scenes lacks momentum, try raising the stakes with a literal or metaphorical "ticking clock".

Epic time

When we say "epic", we're usually describing something huge in scale, monumental. We might be reminded of Greek heroes. Or epic films such as *Jason and the Argonauts* or *Spartacus*, with their vast cinematic landscapes and casts of thousands.

Epic or "epos" comes from ancient Greek literature. It's a long narrative tale – the kind people might have heard round a campfire, told by a bard.

So, the epic was a storytelling genre.

Think: "Once upon a time". Gather round, settle down. You're about to hear a tale.

As the writer of *Beowulf* said: "Hwaet! Listen up!"

Aristotle saw the epic poem as an inferior art form to drama.

A bard who begins: "once upon a time" can take you anywhere. Transport you to a timeless realm and a distant place.

The epic wears its storytelling nature on its sleeve, and doesn't try to hide it. Its freewheeling nature means it's more detached. It can swoop around, like MacKendrick's imaginary winged witness.

For Aristotle, the intimacy of drama made it superior.

In his thinking, tragedy showed events directly, pulling the audience right into the action. It allowed them to experience close-up detail. It was a powerfully direct and immersive way to tell a story. The dramatic unities created even more of a pressure cooker for the audience. They could laugh, cry and quake along with the characters, and ideally experience catharsis.

However, there's no good or bad here. Epic techniques are just another tool in the writer's toolbox.

And epic time is a particular kind of time. It's in stark contrast to the compressed, pressure-cooker time of the dramatic unities. It can stretch over a long, long time. Years, even centuries. With epic time, the storyteller is more detached and godlike. Essentially, you've got a very big effects box. You can use it to transport your audience in both time and space.

So, what's the advantage of epic viewpoint for writers?

Firstly, it's great for orientation and context. You can sketch in big chunks of time with a single sentence. Transport your reader to a different century instantly. Cut between two decades, two years, two weeks. Play with meanwhiles, flashbacks, and moments on a whim.

You can save a lot of time. You can cut to the chase.

And you can be more playful. You, the storyteller, are firmly in charge, and don't mind who knows it.

But this comes at a price.

A detached viewpoint means more emotional detachment. The reader is in the same godlike position as the storyteller, as if they're looking down on the story from a height. In a sense, they're outside time, transcending it.

Instead of inside lived, immersive action.

Which might be something you prefer. It's up to you to make that call.

If this all sounds familiarly like "show" and "tell" here, you're right.

Most writers know about the distinction between detached and immersive viewpoints. But you may not have considered how it relates to epic time.

"Show/tell" isn't just about viewpoint, or spatial distance. It's also about time.

Imagining time

As writers, we're so used to experiencing and manipulating time that we scarcely notice it. We take it in our stride, as a normal part of storytelling.

However, our handling of time is extraordinary. Time is highly elastic, and can be stretched, chopped, compressed, run backwards, and shunted around in amazing ways.

We're so steeped in this normality that it can be hard to step back, and look at what's really going on.

So, it can be helpful to use visual metaphors. For example, camera lenses:

Epic time is like looking through a telephoto lens. Think: *distant mountains, the dots of people far away*.

Real time is like a 50mm camera lens, close to normal human vision. Think: *someone next to you in a room*.

Slow motion is like a close-up or macro lens. Think: *a long look at a glint of dew on a leaf*.

Another great metaphor for imagining time, especially at scene level, is the video editor.

In a video editing screen, we see time laid out as a long ribbon. This is a useful reflection of the linear metaphor of time as a road, stretching out in front and behind. But it also lets you imagine chopping, shunting and stretching time, just as you can do in storytelling.

In video editing, you can also compress the ribbon to see an entire film at once: epic view. Or you can stretch it, to a long, lingering moment. And in between, you can see the familiar pace of everyday realism.

As a storyteller, you're in charge of time. It's one of your tools for shaping your audience's experience. So, it's good to have a bold and robust understanding of how it works.

Bearing in mind this powerful "time ribbon" metaphor, let's look at the different kinds of time. Understanding time in movies, and why people make certain choices, really helps with editing fiction. I'll start with real time, which is closest to "normal vision".

Real time

In "real time" film, the story timeframe is the same as real world audience time. So, the audience experiences an hour-long story in an hour. There are no flashbacks, slow motion, or speeding up.

In stage plays, real time performances are relatively common. A play lasting half an hour is often a single scene, a "slice of life". You don't get the fast cutting typical of film.

But in movies, real time stories are unusual.

The few mainstream examples include *Run Lola Run, High Noon*, and *12 Angry Men*. In each of these, the audience experiences real time unfolding. Mostly, though, real-time movies are art house or experimental, such as *Russian Ark*, which was also filmed in a single take.

In recent years, real-time action has become popular in "slow television". These are restful documentaries showing moment-by-moment footage of a quiet activity, with no cuts. They include

50

a train journey, a wood fire burning, a sleigh ride. This style of film originated in Norway and is strangely compelling! I started watching a sleigh ride, thinking I'd dip in for a minute or two, and found myself completely drawn into that snowy reindeer world.

But for most audiences, real-time pace without cuts is too slow.

So, most movies are made of chopped chunks of the time ribbon, cut together. So time is compressed by cutting out the boring bits.

And mostly, the remaining chunks are in real time.

There are two exceptions: slow motion, and fast motion.

Slowing time

Slow motion footage can happen at different speeds. Often, it's only slightly slower than real life, as in a sports action replay. Sometimes, you see extreme "bullet time" - an ultra-slow visual effect you may have seen in *The Matrix*.

Although the technique is called "slow motion", you're not just slowing movement. You're also slowing the audience's experience of time.

Slow motion is used to draw attention to an important moment that would otherwise pass in a flash.

Often, it's chosen for crucial story moments that would be disappointingly short in real time. For example, the death of the hero, the winning goal, the fall from the cliff-top.

And it's not just so that the audience can savour the cinematography, or the expression on the protagonist's face.

It's because they need to experience a satisfying story arc. We need time to witness and process that story moment, and its implications. If it's over too quickly, we won't feel satisfaction or catharsis.

Slow motion is a way to foreground this kind of story-critical moment, by stretching time.

51

Sometimes, slow-motion footage is critical to the entire meaning of the film. Without it, the whole emotional journey would disintegrate.

Imagine the end of *Butch Cassidy and the Sundance Kid* with the two men bolting from their hiding-place, and getting gunned down in a second.

Imagine the end of *Thelma and Louise* with the car smashing instantly to the ground, with the two women inside.

People don't want realism in these iconic film moments. Who wants to see their heroes and heroines die sudden, violent deaths?

Rather, we want to see the final truth of the *story arc*, about independent spirits who do things their own way. Showing their deaths in realistic time would send a terrible message about the theme. It would say: "know your limits - let the enemy win".

Instead, with slow motion, we focus on the characters' glorious last bid for freedom. Even though their enemies have closed in and there's no way out, they know the ultimate independence of choosing their own death.

These slow motion shots let the story play out in the audience's minds, and resonate long after the end of the film. They create the illusion of a continuing trajectory, rather than the more truthful, brutal, alternative.

The strange time-stretching of slow motion can be put to other uses, too. For example, it's often used to evoke altered states of perception. The "bullet time" in *The Matrix* simulates Neo's otherworldly viewpoint. The slow-motion sequences in *Dredd* show the effect of using the drug, Slo-Mo.

Foregrounding

Slow motion is one way to slow time, by stretching it out on the time ribbon. But you can also slow time by drawing focused attention to something, in what's known as "foregrounding". If a writer spends a long time showing us something, we assume it's important to the story.

Say you provide a long, lingering shot of the villain's bright blue tie. You're saying: "Spend time considering that tie!" Maybe it's a clue for the detective? Or a warning for the victim? It's not just random costume.

Or, say you provide an extended shot of a mountain landscape. We're invited to breathe in its atmosphere, get to know it. You're saying: "This isn't just any story. It's a mountain story."

Of course, everything you show is important at some level. Every word is chosen for a reason.

But when you devote more time to something, you're planting a flag that says: "Pay attention!"

Foregrounding is the acting of drawing attention to something, increasing its salience. And at the same time, fading what's less important into the background, or cutting it entirely.

It's like tuning a radio, to clarify the important signal and tone down the crackly background noise.

Foregrounding creates clarity, and stops confusion. We know where the main focus is meant to be.

The opposite of foregrounding is a collage of stuff, where nothing really stands out. This can feel confusing and overwhelming to the reader.

If you're an experimental writer, this may be OK. You may be trying to explore consciousness, or alienation, or anti-narrative. The French "new novel" (*nouveau roman*) played with reader expectations in this way.

But if you're a storyteller, you'll need to provide clear signals and less noise. Readers want to know where to put their attention.

So, you need to shape the ebb and flow of time, by giving prominence to what's important, and less to what doesn't matter so much.

Film visualization comes in really handy here.

When you're writing, think of time as elastic. You can manipulate it to emphasize what the reader needs to know.

For example, have they spent enough time with the blood-encrusted knife? Or have you skated over it too quickly? Have you buried it in the middle of a paragraph?

Don't bury a crucial clue in a morass of words, where it might be missed.

If it's important, give it a new paragraph, to set it apart visually. Give it some detail, to prolong the time the reader spends with it.

The same applies to any important element of your story, whether it's the hero's outsize feet, the heroine's scar, the murder weapon.

Tune up the story signal, tune down the noise. Pick out what really counts, and give it more air time.

Time sequence

When you're writing and editing, you also need to control how time is arranged, its sequence. In real life, some impacts hit us before others.

For example, if there are burning tyres at the crime scene, this would probably hit your senses from a good distance. Well before any sounds or visual information.

As you move closer, the smell might be so strong that you struggle to breathe.

And eventually, you'll get close enough to see the tyres, and notice that they're tractor tyres. And closer still, they're scruffy and covered in mud.

Don't tell the reader first about the charred heaps of tyres, then tell us about the stench a page later.

To bring a scene to life, think of its order of impact in reality. Arrange those impacts in a logical sequence. This can help you to foreground what needs to be prominent for the story.

Crucially, it will help to immerse your reader in the character's viewpoint.

Speeding up time

Speeded-up movie footage (fast-mo) is much rarer than slo-mo. It's typically used for comedy, as in *The Three Stooges*. Like slo-mo, it can also be used to show altered perceptions or alienation, as in Scarlett Johansson's drugged character in the movie *Lucy*.

Mostly, however, time in film is speeded up using cuts.

By cutting from one scene to the next, the director leaves out anything static or boring. That leaves only footage that moves the story along.

Remember the metaphor of time as a long ribbon? With cuts, the editor chops away the dull or unwanted stuff, and shunts the remaining chunks or "shots" together.

These shots are essentially mini chunks of time and space.

Small chunks of time can be shunted together to create scenes. Then scenes and sequences of scenes are shunted together to create stories. For more about these bigger blocks of time, check out the sections on *Scene* and *Sequence*.

If you're writing or editing a novel, film editing conventions can be really helpful. This is because film editing handles time in a bold way, which is helpful for structural editing.

Think of scenes as beads in a necklace. But beads don't need string to link them together. They can simply be juxtaposed. For example:

A farmer is going to harvest a field of wheat, early in the morning. You don't need to show him waking up, getting ready, walking to his vehicle, driving to the field. You can do this with two shots:

> *The farmer is woken up by a loud alarm clock.*
> *The farmer drives his combine harvester through*
> *the wheat field.*

Our minds fill in the rest. Our brains are wonderful story-making machines. They're very good at making sense of disparate elements, of working out cause and effect. We do this even when the two shots are unrelated.

In terms of writing, you can use this technique to cut between scenes without showing the "travel" in between. Simply end one scene, leave a couple of paragraph lines to signal a change of scene, and begin the new one.

As long as you plant clear enough signposts, the reader will follow.

This means, for example, making sure you use character names and pronouns clearly at the start of the new scene, so that readers know which character they're with. And if you take them to an entirely new place, then we need a word or two to establish context.

In many ways, cutting to a new scene is like the start of a new story. Initial signposts needs especial care.

Cuts on rising action

Film editing has another trick up its sleeve that's useful for fiction writers: cutting a scene on "rising action".

Rising action is when a scene is gathering pace and energy, rather than slowing down. Or there's a question in the audience's mind, but not yet an answer. So it's a bit like a hook.

Think of rising action as a wave which is going to crest and then tumble onward.

For example: the heroine runs to her flat, fumbles with the key, hears the phone ringing inside. Who's calling? Is it urgent? This is rising action.

Then, she runs inside, grabs the phone. It's her friend. This is falling action.

The action has peaked, because the questions have been answered.

But if you cut the end of a scene on rising action, the question keeps resonating in our minds, and acts as a hook. It encourages us to read on.

Check out the ends of your scenes. See whether they suggest forward momentum, or reach a point of rest and closure. Small changes here can make a big difference to the reader's engagement, and perception of pace.

Montage

Montage is another way to edit time. It's deep in the DNA of film technique.

The word montage simply means "assembly", and refers to a group of shots cut together. The early Soviet film directors, Sergei Eisenstein and Lev Kuleshov, brought montage to prominence. They spotted the power of assembling shots to create new meanings and collisions, and also to wrangle place and time.

One very common use of montage is to show compressed passage of time. It's often used to show long durational events that might otherwise be dull on film.

For example, say you want to show your protagonist learning how to box. It would be pretty dull to show the minute details of his training. Instead, you'd compile a montage of key moments: pulling on gloves, getting punched, skipping, getting fitter, tougher, until the moment when the protagonist is ready for the important story moment: the big fight scene.

Or, say you want to show someone preparing for a big night out. You might show a montage sequence of shower, shave, get dressed, hair, slap on perfume. Then a ring at the doorbell might signal the start of the next scene.

The shots can be in the same place – say, showing someone planting a crop and eventually reaping it. Or they can be in different places. For example, your protagonist is doing door-to-door community work over a week, or a month.

You can even use montage to show the passage of the seasons or years in this way. For example, the changes in a garden. And unlike timelapse, which has thousands of shots cut together, with montage, you only need a few key moments.

We're so used to seeing montage that we often don't notice it as a distinct sequence within the larger film structure. But it's a cornerstone of film storytelling.

What's most helpful for fiction is the realisation that you don't need to show everything that takes place over a long period of time. You can be really bold and cut to the chase. A snapshot of the main character learning to box might be all you need to establish something that takes months. This frees you up to crack on with the story.

Past and present

In fiction, your choice of tense has a big impact on how your story feels for the reader. Fiction is so fluid with time, compared to scripts, that it's easy to wander all over the place, and get lost.

Script time has in-built rigour that can be useful when it comes to structural decisions, and clarity of momentum. And it automatically helps with show and tell.

But first, a reminder of fictional time, starting with present tense. The present is vivid, immersive, active, sometimes voyeuristic. It feels as though the story is unfolding as we watch. Present tense is often used for action thrillers. It's also used in other genres, such as fiction written in diary or letter form.

The main problem with present tense is authenticity.

This might seem paradoxical. After all, present tense puts us right in the middle of the action, witnessing it first-hand. That's surely a front row seat!

But if the character is in the middle of the action, how are they managing to speak to us? If they're walking through the park or leaping across rooftops, how are they finding time to tell us what they're doing? And why?

Of course, readers are good at suspending disbelief to enjoy a great story. They often forgive a lack of plausibility, as long as the ride is entertaining. And it might be they're using present tense to narrate the past, as you might do down the pub, when you're painting a vivid picture:

> *I'm walking through the park. It's freezing cold.*
> *Ice on the path. The sun's setting. Suddenly,*
> *this huge guy comes bearing down on me from*
> *nowhere. "What the hell are you doing?"*

This use of present tense occupies an intriguing space in our heads, between past and present, mixing a flavour of both. So present tense can be an extremely versatile and evocative technique in fiction.

But the more typical mode of fiction is the past tense.

> *He was walking through the park. It was freezing*
> *cold. Ice on the path. The sun was setting.*
> *Suddenly, this huge guy came bearing down from*
> *nowhere. "What the hell are you doing?"*

In fiction, the predominance of the past tense makes sense. A narrator is usually in a storytelling relationship to the action, describing something that has already happened. Implicitly, the narrator has come out the other side, got their breath back, and gained enough distance to put pen to paper.

But in film and stage drama, the dominant mode is the lived present. The present is the element that dramatic stories live in. Even if the material is historical, we're still seeing the action physically unfold before us. We witness the lived present of the characters.

It follows, then, that the past needs to be handled differently.

Note: although each chunk of time shows present action, how the chunks are woven together into a story can be wildly non-linear. The chronology can jump back and forward with just as much complexity as in fiction.

The movies of directors such as David Lynch and Quentin Tarantino play in a very sophisticated way with time, moving chunks of it about without the familiar logic of conventional movies. This can work brilliantly in thrillers, where audiences are trying to piece together a puzzle. It can also be used to unsettling effect, to create a fragmented sense of the characters' reality.

However, this kind of movie is at the extreme end of time-wrangling, and a more linear chronology is more typical.

Looking at movie time structures can help us to appreciate the flexibility enjoyed by fiction writers. It's so easy to play fast and loose with time in fiction that writers often don't notice they're doing it.

For example:

> The garden was a mess, though last year's
> daffodils were showing signs of life.

This looks fairly simple and clear as a sentence, but in terms of time wrangling, it's highly sophisticated. The phrase "last year's daffodils" catapults us into the past while still witnessing the present. It's a complex dance between time zones, but our brains are surprisingly capable of understanding it.

We scarcely even notice the complexity, as a fiction voice emulates our usual jump-about way of talking and thinking. Our thought processes are gloriously non-linear.

So, fictional storytelling time is highly elastic, and we can easily slip in moments of exposition and backstory. We don't even need to signal them, pause and go back. We can just tuck them into the middle of a sentence, or allude to them in a word or phrase.

But have you ever found yourself going down a blind alleyway of exposition, or writing whole passages about what happened before this point in the story? Have you ever found the past running away with you, and becoming more interesting than the present story? Or writing extended backstory that intrudes in the present?

If this is the case, you may well be slowing down the pace of your story, and losing readers.

At the very least, you need to know when backstory is useful, and when it can be dropped.

Understanding the more rigorous time chunking needed for drama is a massive help with structural editing. I use it to move scenes around, compress them and see where I've gone overboard, or where crucial moments are under-written.

Understanding time through the lens of movie editing is a great confidence-builder when it comes to bold structural decisions. You may decide that your structure is absolutely right for your story, but you may also get a good steer for tightening or structural editing.

That's because time in scriptwriting is dominantly linear and in large chunks, with a few notable exceptions. Concepts such as flashback, flashforward and frame narratives are also more clearly delineated than in fiction. So it's less forgiving than fiction, and structural decisions have to be clear and bold.

If you get stuck, try film thinking to work out whether you're writing a necessary flashback, a frame, a prologue, or are simply indulgently meandering off-piste.

Flashback

Flashbacks are often used to provide exposition or backstory.

In early Hollywood movies, flashbacks were signaled using visual conventions such as the dissolve - a blurred and sometimes woozy transition between shots.

Nowadays, flashbacks may not be signaled at all. We simply see a new shot. We may need to make our own deductions, and piece the chronology together. Audiences are so sophisticated about stories nowadays that they can follow highly demanding narrative time structures. Movies such as *Memento, One Day*, and *Inception* are mind-blowingly complex, but audiences can still get the general gist.

Long flashbacks can be problematic in film. You need to think about them carefully, and justify them. Sometimes they're seen as a cop-out, and aspiring screenwriters are often advised to cut them where possible. This is an over-simplification, as flashbacks are a vital part of movie vocabulary. But it's good to be aware that they're discussed and scrutinised in this robust way.

The main issue with flashbacks is that they stall the story in the present. This can slow momentum and drive. For the audience, it can feel like an aside that distracts from the main action. If the story is exciting, we're impatient for it to crack on.

The end of a flashback and return to the present can also feel a bit clunky. It's like a hypnotist's "back in the room!" We've been AWOL, and now we've returned. This makes viewers aware of the mechanics of the movie. It can disrupt what would otherwise be an immersive experience. Clearly, you may have very good reasons for including a flashback. But in movies, you wouldn't do it casually, say, as a quick way to introduce exposition.

The same is true for fiction. For example, you might want to dive into your character's childhood story, or show a scene from their mafia past. If this happens mid-story, take a long, hard look at it.

Does it really work in the middle of the story? Or would it be better at the beginning, as a prologue? Or not at all?

Often, a loop of exposition like this can be excised like a burr, with no great loss. Or, if it's vital to the story, it may be better at the start, as a prologue, where it won't disturb the onward momentum.

In the middle of a novel, short flashbacks and chunks of exposition can often work better than full chapters. They're less obtrusive and can fit in with the flow. Watch out for flashbacks that are so long that they dominate the present action. If the backstory is so fascinating that it threatens to usurp the present, maybe that's the stronger story!

When I'm doing structural editing, I keep an eye on domineering flashbacks, by using a highlighter pen to mark up the past and present passages. This helps to show the balance between strands. It makes it easier to decide what to cut down, and what to emphasize.

In movies, it's rare to see flashback just for simple exposition. Why go to the bother of setting up a new scene, when a skilful writer can tuck the information into the script, and keep the momentum going?

Flashbacks can be far more interesting than that. They can be playful, and raise questions about whose "truth" they show.

For example, a crime movie might show a troubling second of terror, or a collage of disturbing images. Is this the objective truth of what happened? Or is it from the character's viewpoint? Is it a memory from someone's inner life, or a vision of what might happen in the future (a flashforward)?

You often see this technique in psychological thrillers, where it can open up fascinating questions of what's real, and what's just in the character's mind.

This ambiguity is achieved by using unexplained cuts, so leaving the audiences compelled to join the dots. Puzzles like this are a kind of imaginative gap, creating intrigue and helping audiences to engage with the story.

In fiction, you can replicate this technique by opening a chapter with a terrifying sequence, plunging the readers into a world of chaos or horror. Then your character comes to. It's been a dream, a memory or a panic attack. An "out of time" jolt like this is a powerful way to dramatize someone's inner life.

In psychological thrillers such as *Memento*, complex non-linear timelines are often used to great effect. The structure echoes the character's confusion and memory loss. *Inception* uses nested narratives, a bit like Russian dolls, to create disturbing layers, and unsettle our sense of reality.

Framed time

Sometimes, a flashback sequence is so long that it's the main meat of the film. *Titanic*, for example, has short "bookends" with elderly Rose at the start and end, with most of the movie in flashback.

63

In this structure, "older Rose" is a frame narrative around the main story about "young Rose". Think of it as a picture frame with its own shape and colour, with a different image inside. There's a clear contrast between the storytelling frame and the story inside it.

This time structure puts us in a distinct relationship to the story. In a sense, we already know how it ends. After all, Rose has survived to tell the tale. So the story isn't about "will she, won't she make it?" The audience knows she's a Titanic survivor. So it's not about "what happens to Rose". It's about "how did she survive?" This narrative frame gives the audience a sense of detachment – a certain distance.

Sometimes, a writer reveals a narrative frame right at the end of the story. The whole story is "reframed" by what we're told at the end.

This is similar to a "twist" ending. As in, the main character wakes up from a dream, or turns out to be a dog.

But twists have a bad reputation and are sometimes seen as old-fashioned and clichéd. Readers can feel cheated, too.

That's because the writer has asked readers to invest time and emotions in getting to know the characters, then pulled the rug from under them. If the story is thin, then it's just a technical trick. It draws attention to the fact that the writer is toying with the reader. Not all readers are impressed by this.

But if the reframe is deeply linked to the theme, and the characters rich and compelling, the effect can be devastating.

Spoiler alert: This reframing technique is used to stunning effect in the Ian McEwan novel and movie adaptation, *Atonement*. It's also used in the Lionel Shriver novel and movie, *We Need to Talk About Kevin*. It's well worth reading these.

The shock of reframing completely overturns our understanding of the story and the characters. It jolts us profoundly, and invites us to read again, with the benefit of hindsight. Read those books! They show a bold and fascinating way of handling time.

Another example of time-framing, maybe surprisingly, is the voiceover. The movie *Out of Africa* opens with the voiceover line,

"I had a farm in Africa". This puts the narrator in the present now, perhaps talking to an imagined someone. And the action of the movie is in the past. It's part of the memories she's looking back on. It's not unusual for film adaptations of novels to include a lot of voiceover. It's one way of dealing with the inner voice.

Sometimes, voiceover isn't framing the past. It's part of the present. For example, many of Woody Allen's films include voiceover commentary on the present action. This technique is often used for comedic effect, to show the gap between a character's reality, and their inner life.

It's worth being aware of these differences. Although they sound similar and are achieved technically in the same way, they're entirely different time structures. They put the audience and characters in a very different relationship to the story.

How might you use this understanding in fiction? One way is to clarify your narrator's time relationship to the story.

Fiction narration is so fluid and relatively forgiving that it can be easy to write without deciding on the narrator's position. Is he or she elderly, speaking about events from fifty years ago? Are they talking about something that happened last week? Are events unfolding as they speak, and changing under them?

If a lot of time has passed, what has happened in the intervening years? Why are they telling this story only now? What has taken them so long? What is compelling them, putting them under pressure to get this story out, today of all days?

These questions can help you to understand your time structure, and prime your stories and narrators with a greater sense of urgency. Narrators tell stories for compelling reasons, so if they're telling a past story, it'll be stronger if you can give it a reason in the present.

This is particularly useful for endings. For example, when we return to "older Rose" in *Titanic*, the story picks up and moves on in the present.

Returning to the outer frame can provide an extra epilogue to extend the story. It gives readers the satisfaction of circularity and closure, along with a sense that life is moving on.

It brings us back to the "pressure cooker" idea of time in dramatic writing. Why today, of all days? Why are you telling this story now?

Naturally, fiction has its own powerful techniques and preferences. But you may find, as I've done, that the robust time structures of scriptwriting are a huge help with objective, confident structural editing.

TRY THIS:

Practise analysing the time structures of the stories you encounter. Tip: start with movies, as their structures are often more straightforward.

Are the stories real-time linear, or frame narratives? Is there a prologue or epilogue? Do they use flashbacks, flashforwards, or other playful ways with time? Are there any dream sequences or visions? Montages? Slow motion?

How many narrative strands are there (sometimes called A, B and C stories)? Are these strands simultaneous, or time displaced?

Then, create a simplified visual of the story's timeline.

Try this for a few different books and movies. What do you notice? Do you have any preferences? What kinds of story structure engage you, and what kinds lose your interest?

TRY THIS:

When you do a structural edit on your work in progress, mark up or highlight the past and present sections, to show where time shifts. Also mark where the narration goes into expositional asides, or "epic" storytelling.

Then, in Word or another text editor, click View/Multiple Pages to shrink the pages and see the whole book at once. This can help to reveal the balance between exposition and present action, narration and dramatization.

You can also use colours to highlight different narrator strands, or point-of-view shifts. Scrivener lets you do this with colour coding in Outline view, which is incredibly useful.

TRY THIS:

When you're doing a line edit, print out a section of your novel, story or poem, and highlight time signposts.

Time signposts can include past, present and future verbs, and words such as then, since, before, as, after.

What do you discover about the timeline? How would you describe it?

Is your timeline fragmented and complex? Or straight linear?

Do you find it hard to spot the time jumps? Are they fictionally fluid, or clear cut? Time travel in a poem can shift very quickly, even in individual words and phrases. What do you discover about the temporal flow of your writing?

Do you have any habitual time structures, such as starting lots of sentences with as or while, or -ing forms of the verb? What impact do your choices have on pace and clarity? How might they affect the reader in different ways?

TRY THIS:

Try line editing using a passage from an author you admire, marking up their work to get a sense of their temporal footprint.

What do you discover about their handling of time? Does anything surprise you? What techniques can you learn for your own writing?

See also: Scene, Wants and Stakes, Show and Tell, Transformation, Catharsis.

67

Dramatic Action

Dramatic action is all about wants, stakes, and the work of the influential theatre director Stanislavski. This book has separate chapters covering these in detail.

But here's an overview to give context, and explain why dramatic action isn't as obvious as you might think.

Dramatic action doesn't mean sword-swishing, murders, hysterics and car chases, though it can, of course, mean all those things.

It's best to understand "dramatic action" as a technical term. It means a certain kind of action engineered to have built-in drive, tension and momentum. The kind that advances the plot and character relationships, and signals meaningful change.

Dramatic action is never just action for action's sake. It's always loaded with important meaning for the characters.

It always involves vital character decisions and turning points.

It's always in the service of the story.

And as a by-product, it will engage the audience emotionally, and keep them on the edge of their seats.

Why are car chases dramatically boring?

It's not just me, is it? I've done a quick unscientific straw poll, and all the people I asked agreed: car chases are boring.

One even said: "A car chase is when I go and put the kettle on."

Yes! Even with mammoth budgets and full-on mayhem, chicken-scattering, red-light-smashing, gravel-squealing and motorway pile-ups, car chases are still unexciting.

Why, with all that budget flung at wonderful spectacular effects, is this so?

It's partly because we know the ending. The protagonist is likely to survive, and there's nothing really, truly at stake to keep us interested.

It's also because car chases are typically just spectacle. Visually amazing, but essentially high-octane filler. According to Aristotle, spectacle was the least important dramatic element.

Car chases also come with a built-in problem: how to keep building more and more "wow" factor. Audiences can very quickly get jaded with "wow", and expect bigger and bigger thrills. And it's impossible to fulfil that expectation.

But even more fundamentally, car chases are boring because their dramatic action is limited.

A typical car chase often has just one dramatic action, spun out into a long sequence. Usually, it's something like:

Someone hunts down someone else.

There are variations, but that's the basic structure and drive of the scene. Emotionally, it's more or less linear. It doesn't have enough twists and turns to keep the audience strongly engaged.

The escalating events all play the same kind of emotional note.

Yes, there's mounting spectacle, ever-bigger crashes, ever more touch-and-go brushes with death. But those are escalations. They're not reversals, or changes in underlying drive or intention.

For a story to come truly to life, it needs twists and turns, shifts in power, status and emotional note. Not just escalations or different kinds of obstacle.

For dramatic interest, the protagonist needs to experience change.

The "question of the scene"

The question of the scene is a technique for thinking about tension and hooks. Many scriptwriters use it to structure their scenes.

Simply establish a question in the minds of the audience, and chain questions together to create a journey. From the audience viewpoint, you'll be pulled along by curiosity, wanting to find out the answers to the questions.

For example, the restaurant worker returns late at night to their flat. While they're unlocking the door, they hear a noise inside.

At that moment, the writer has planted the question:

Is someone inside the flat?

And the audience won't be satisfied until the question has been answered – whether the cat jumps out from the curtain, or the murderer leaps from the dark.

The question and its answer form a kind of arc. Knowledge is withheld, to hook the audience's curiosity.

You'll often come across scene questions such as:

Is she going to tell him?
Will he find the key?
Will that bomb go off? (literally or metaphorically)

With this technique, scenes can be broken down further into a chain of mini-questions.

For example, a scene might start with an ominous floorboard creak. Question:

What's that noise?

Once the audience gets their answer (Aha! The cat behind the door!), they need a new question:

Why is that light on?

And so on. Having a clear chain of questions like this will help you to keep the story moving. It's another way of looking at beats, if you like.

For example, let's look at a car chase sequence. Often, a car chase is a set piece, and has just one dramatic question or arc:

Will the protagonist achieve their goal?

So, you could break this into mini-questions:

Will the protagonist avoid the oncoming lorry?
Will they get through the overturned market stalls?
Will they shake off the chickens and straw bales and keep going?

However, one thing to watch out for is the element of surprise. All these questions play the same kind of emotional note. They're escalations of the same thing.

Yes, there's mounting spectacle, ever-bigger crashes, ever more touch-and-go brushes with death. But they're not reversals, or changes in underlying drive or dramatic action.

For a story to come truly to life, it needs twists and turns, not just escalations or different kinds of obstacle. So, you need to consider how you can keep things surprising.

One way to do this is to use the rule of threes. Twice is a pattern. The protagonist zooms past the oncoming lorry, the overturned market stalls. The third obstacle, the chicken and straw bales, are more of the same. What different emotion could you introduce, the third time?

Maybe the sidekick pulls a gun and turns out to be an enemy. Maybe the car fills with choking fumes. Maybe the protagonist's phone rings and it's her kid.

Check that your third beat isn't just an escalation. Make it a twist. Otherwise, the question and answer technique can become too samey. The most spectacular car chase can become "movement", rather than "momentum".

Dramatic action - the beating heart of story

Car chases are an example of a kind of scene that often appears dramatic and full of physical action and doing, but has limited dramatic action.

Dramatic actions are the beating heart of drama.

They come from deep within the characters.

Characters who want something so much that they'll go to amazing lengths to get it.

Who are so driven and motivated, they need to take action or burst.

Characters who are under so much pressure, they need to decide. Now.

The joy of dramatic action for audiences is seeing the characters under pressure. Feeling that pressure along with them. Watching what they decide, how they turn, what they do. After all, remember the word drama comes from the ancient Greek for "to do, to act".

Dramatic action allows us to feel the characters' pain, hope, and fear, and live it alongside them, without coming to harm.

So, here's an example:

What's more dramatic?

1. A couple racing their red Lamborghini through the bazaars of Istanbul?

2. A man on the first day at his new job, deciding whether to
   wear his wedding ring?

At first glance, (1) seems far more dramatic. Sports car, exotic
location. Lots of crashing through stalls, screeching round tight
corners. A couple, probably good-looking, escaping from the
villain, or chasing the villain down.

But in terms of dramatic action, the answer is (2). The man at
his new job, deciding whether to wear his wedding ring.

And it's not just because (1) is a trope you've seen many times
before. They're both familiar scenarios.

So what's the difference with Wedding Ring Man? It's a decision
point for the character. The action he takes at that critical point
will speak volumes.

Will we see him twirl the ring on his finger, think about it, then
deliberately, coldly, take it off, and shut it in a drawer?

Or, will we see him put on the ring with a sigh?

His decision will set in motion the next chain of events.
Crucially, we see him decide.

Whereas with the Lamborghini car chase, once the couple are
in the car and on their way, all we really see is spectacle.

Don't get me wrong. Spectacle can be wonderful. I'm a sucker
for the James Bond films, with their glorious chase sequences:
down ski slopes and twisty mountain roads, along the Thames...
They're cracking great fun to watch.

But little is really, truly at stake.

Actions

Actors and directors use the concept of "actions" to analyze scenes
and break them down into sections. This approach is sometimes
called "actioning" or "uniting". It's based on the work of the Russian
director, Stanislavski. For more about this, see the chapter on his
work later on.

But in the meantime, here's a useful starting-point. In each scene, the characters need an overall intention. If they're just mooching about aimlessly, talking to each other, they're not dramatic. The only exception here is if there's a dramatic subtext below the mooching. For example, they're pretending to chew the fat, but in reality, they're waiting for the getaway jet ski to arrive.

Dramatic actions have a strong sense of underlying intention. You often hear actors calling it "motivation". And appropriately, the root of motivation is motus: movement, motion, momentum.

Intention is the high-octane fuel that drives the characters forwards.

And action without underlying intention is just movement.

TRY THIS:
Look at the scenes in your work in progress, and identify each character's overall dramatic action. What's the essence of the scene? Do they want to persuade, placate, overcome, or distract the other character? Brainstorm active verbs that express one character's action on the other.

Are the characters in conflict, or are they on the same side? If they're on the same side, where's the tension?

Actions can often be paired into opposites – for example, *persuade/dissuade, focus/distract,* and so on. Looking at the verbs in your list, what are their opposite actions? If you escalate their intensity, or tone them down, what verbs do you get?

Try using your discoveries to amplify the differences between your characters.

See also: Stanislavski, Wants and Stakes, Beats, Catharsis, Obligatory Scene, Iglesias.

Further reading:
Caldarone, M. and Lloyd-Williams, M. (2017) *Actions: The Actors' Thesaurus.* London, Nick Hern.

Tension

"Plays are all about tension," says the eminent British playwright, David Edgar.

"Plays are like bicycles. If they aren't going somewhere, they're falling over," says the equally eminent radio dramatist, Mike Walker.

Tension is at the heart of the other story genres, too.

Imagine a coiled spring imprisoned between your fingers.

When you let it go, it has to leap away, in a mini explosion of movement. It's designed that way. It has no choice.

A dramatic script operates along the same principle.

If you, the writer, can build in tension from the start, the story will have no choice but to unleash its momentum, and leap forth.

Dramatic action is all about building in tightly coiled tension at the start, so that the story can motor under its own momentum.

There are many different ways to create dramatic tension. They include secrets, conflict, transformations, dramatic irony and many other tools covered in this book.

Note that dramatic tension isn't the same as everyday physical tension - the shoulder-crunching, jaw-clenching kind you might feel after a stressful day.

Like dramatic action, it has inherent momentum that comes from character drives and situational pressures.

Create tension in your writing, and your readers or audience will experience tension, too. And hopefully, they'll stay around to feel the moment when it resolves.

Now, test yourself.

Which is an example of dramatic tension?

1. A man unable to sleep in the night for worry about losing his job?
2. A woman at a dinner party when her secret lover arrives unexpectedly?

In the first example, the sleepless man, he's clearly full of tension. Things might get worse for him in the morning, when he goes to work and finds his desk already cleared.

But fraught dinner party has more dramatic tension, because the whole scene is overshadowed by a huge secret between the characters. The scene is essentially "primed" with this knowledge.

To make the scene even tenser, give the audience the same knowledge. Let them know that the new arrival is the lover. Then, the whole scene is underlaid with a powerful subtext and lots of questions.

Does anyone else know they're lovers? Did the lover know she was going to be there? Will they let the truth slip? How can she stop her heart from pounding fit to burst?

Then, try upping the ante with a "ticking clock":

> *What if the secret lover is fed up pretending, drinks too much and looks like he'll spill the beans?*

You'll have the audience on the edge of their seats.

When the audience knows more than the characters, it's called "dramatic irony". It's one of the most powerful ways of creating tension in a script. It creates an emotional charge between the characters, or between characters and audience.

76

TRY THIS:

Check your scenes to see whether they have enough built-in tension between the characters.

Are they both on the same side, or too collusive or friendly to each other?

Are they talking about someone else who's not in the room?

Do they want opposite things strongly?

Is something at stake if they don't get what they want?

If not, check out some of the upcoming dramatic techniques for creating tension.

TRY THIS:

Tension is aligned to pace, though not the same thing. Tension is more like a strong undertow current deep down in the sea. Whereas pace is more like the rhythm of the surface waves.

Once you've created underlying tension in your scene, check that the pace serves the tension, too.

For example, do you have lots of exposition and backstory which is stalling the story?

Do your scene cuts end on rising action, or on a sense of rest? What works best for your story and genre?

Do the lengths of your sentences and paragraphs create the right pace at the right time? Try the effect of breaking them up to foreground key moments.

Visual layout also helps to reinforce pace. Long paragraphs tend to be slower-paced and reflective. Dialogue and short paragraphs typically have more momentum. Both can be used to create tension in different ways. In print books, page-turning can also be used to create tension. For example, you can ask a question and delay the answer until the next page.

Experiment with different sentence, paragraph and visual layouts to explore the effect on tension.

See also: Secrets, Dramatic Action, Dramatic Irony, Time, Scene, Catharsis, Fatal Flaw, Iglesias.

Scene

A scene is the basic unit of drama, in a similar way to chapters and paragraphs being basic units of fiction.

In dramatic technique, scenes are the building blocks of story.

It can be helpful to think of scenes as beads that are strung together. Each one is a discrete chunk of space and time.

In film and TV scriptwriting, scenes don't usually have smooth transitions in between. Instead, one scene simply cuts or dissolves to the next.

Viewers now understand these techniques so intuitively that we take them for granted.

But when film makers started out, these cuts were revolutionary.

The first major narrative film maker, Georges Meliès, had a theatre background. So, his films were set in a theatre space, with theatrical drapes and props. He used a fixed camera, and his scenes were relatively long, with characters and props moving around.

Later, film makers discovered a new technique of moving the camera, and cutting sharply between scenes.

The effect of this was to compress time and space.

Say you wanted to show your character - let's call her "Kay" - going for an important job interview.

You could show Kay getting ready, dressing smartly, leaving the house, shutting the door. You could show her getting into her car, and the minute stages of her journey, until the moment when she sits in front of the interview panel.

Or you could simply show her:

- leaving the house in her smart clothes
- arriving at the workplace
- sitting in front of the panel.

You could even miss out her arrival at the office! Our storytelling minds are great at working out cause and effect, and can easily deduce what's in between.

Note that this cutting technique compresses both time and space. Kay's house and the office building could be hundreds of miles apart, but the cut creates an illusion that they're together. In the real world of movie shooting, they might also be miles apart, but again, the viewer completely buys the illusion that they're next to each other.

If you've ever seen a movie shot in a familiar city, you'll often spot places cut together that are far apart in real life.

If scenes and shots are skilfully cut together, the audience joins the dots, without an explanatory transition.

So, what's useful about this for fiction? You don't need to show all the stages of a story, or the glue that links the flow together.

You can simply cut to the next scene.

This can be done at the ends of chapters, or at the ends of sections. For example:

She seized the shotgun, and headed out into the woods.

What the character does next is: she treks for hours through the woods, stumbles on branches, gets hungry, the light falling. Then she reaches the cottage.

However, you don't need to write all this. You can simple write:

> *She seized the shotgun, and headed out into the*
> *woods.*

Then:

> *It was dark as she reached the cottage. Craig's*
> *battered jeep was parked by the door. The kitchen*
> *light shone a square onto the gravel. He'd have*
> *fired up the wood stove by now. Probably frying*
> *something vile he'd picked up off the road.*
> *She heaved the gun from her aching shoulder.*

The cut works because the end of the cut signals the forward direction of travel:

> *She seized the shotgun, and headed out into the*
> *woods.*

Then the new scene picks it up again, establishes the new setting quickly:

> *It was dark as she reached the cottage.*

The new scene also has several elements that quickly help us to follow the flow:

- ❀ the pronoun *she* stays consistent
- ❀ passage of time is indicated with *it was dark*
- ❀ the end of the journey is signaled with *reached the cottage*
- ❀ the place is sketched in, for a clearer mind's eye picture. There's context (she reached the cottage) and some detail (Craig's battered jeep was parked by the door). Both together help to set the picture.
- ❀ a clear viewpoint. Free indirect style is used to align us with the protagonist's thoughts: *He'd have fired up the wood*

80

stove by now. Note: it's also past perfect, quickly sketching in the recent past.

❈ the end of the cut is connected to the new scene with the help of a linking object: the gun.

These elements all help to ease the transition.

You might not need so much signposting, but this a useful checklist.

You could also draw the reader along in a more oblique way that teases and intrigues more. For example:

> *Bloody shoulder. She swore as it sent another bolt of pain through her neck. Last time it had been this bad, she'd gulped painkillers like they were sweets. But the last dusty pill she'd found in her pocket had worn off hours ago.*
> *She shrugged, testing the limits of her arm movement. Another stab of pain.*
> *But she could still lift the gun, and rest the muzzle on a branch.*
> *That branch right there, for example. Perfect line of sight to the kitchen window.*

This draws us into the same scene. And it links to the previous scene by expanding a single element before the cut: the protagonist's painful shoulder.

It doesn't try to draw in all the elements early on. Instead, it starts with a narrow focus and gradually pulls out to build a picture. It's a similar technique to the "closeup then pull out to wide" technique discussed earlier.

By focusing close on the shoulder, the reader will be asking questions: Where is she? What's going on? - before you pull out to reveal the new setting.

With this technique, you need to find a good balance: enough mystery to intrigue, but not so much that you confuse the reader.

Choosing a single element to focus on and develop helps to keep the flow clear.

In this example, there was only one narrative viewpoint, so keeping the focus is fairly straightforward.

But many novels have two or three viewpoint strands, and switch between narrators. It means you need even more care with signposting. As long as you signal clearly that the perspective has changed, and orientate your reader quickly, they'll cog with your story and follow along.

With multiple viewpoints, some situations need extra special care. For example, in alternate chapters:

- With two same-sex characters, the pronouns he and she can get detached from their characters. You may need to repeat names more often, to keep everything clear.
- Gender-neutral or similar-sounding names can make it harder to "see" distinctive characters quickly. This is true also with names of a similar length, or implied age or social status. It's best to keep names distinct from each other on as many dimensions as possible.
- In science fiction and fantasy, you're writing a new world with few easy reference points for orientation. So you need more signposts.

Extra attention to the openings and orientation in these situations will help your readers to follow more easily.

Ending scenes on rising action

The ends of scenes can also be used to increase tension and hook the audience's attention along.

In fast-paced movies, editors typically cut on a moment of rising action, rather than rest.

That's because if the characters are in stasis – for example, sitting on a sofa - there's no momentum to pull us into the next scene.

If they're in action but the action is complete - say, they've hammered the lid on the tea chest filled with gold - then the energy has fallen.

Cutting in the middle of the action - while they're still hammering down the lid - keeps it alive and in progress in our minds.

Our brains experience a phenomenon called the Zeigarnik effect - the need to feel a sense of completion. Incomplete actions are like tiny irritants which occupy our minds in a state of subtle tension.

By denying us a sense of closure, a writer or editor can hold us in tension, leaving us hanging on in, to experience the outcome.

So, cutting on rising action is a powerful technique for keeping readers reading, and audiences watching.

Look at the ends of your chapter sections and see if you can sharpen them up, leaving the characters on a point of rising action.

For example:

> She seized the shotgun, and headed out into the
> woods.

is more dynamic than:

> She packed her rucksack, laid the shotgun on the
> table, and went to bed.
> She'd head out into the woods in the morning.

In the second example, the writer needs to get the protagonist up and out of the house in the morning.

It probably isn't an exciting part of the story - unless you plan to wake up the protagonist with a bump in the night.

Note: if you use cuts on rising action, don't overdo it. It can become a tic.

And don't signal a cliffhanger by using "dot dot dot", as in:

> *She seized the shotgun, and headed out into the*
> *woods...*

It's like waving a huge flag that says: "Suspense ahoy!". It's unsubtle, and draws attention to your author tricks, jolting the reader out of the story. It's like using exclamation marks to laugh at your own jokes. Use them very sparingly.

TRY THIS:

Check your scene openings. Do they open on a point of action, or something more restful, such as reflection or description?

Do your chapter openings have a good variety of mood and pace?

Next, read them together with the scene ending just before. Do the endings make you want to read on? Are the signposts clear?

Explore different kinds of "camera" shots for your chapter and section openings. See if you can find intriguing ways in which to arouse curiosity, or plant a question.

TRY THIS:

To edit scenes, try using a fluorescent highlighter pen, or different font colours.

Highlighting each scene in a different colour helps you see how long each chunk of the story is. It also helps you to spot narrative changes, such as different character viewpoints.

I find this helicopter view of structure really helpful. It often shows up where I've skimped on an important moment, or where a key story moment is missing.

I also use highlighters within scenes. This helps me to see shifts in time, such as back-flips, asides, and exposition where the present story stalls. It helps to show whether they're all earning their keep, or just holding up the momentum.

The first time I did this for my fiction in progress, I was shocked to see how little of my writing was present action, and how much was excursions into the past.

If you're writing literary or experimental fiction, scene-based thinking may not be helpful. You might prefer the complex time-weaving that's possible with prose.

But in most kinds of storytelling, scene analysis and thinking in a filmic way can help you to pick up pace and make more confident editing decisions.

See also: Show and Tell, Obligatory Scene, Space, Beat, Sequence.

Beats

The word "beat" has several different meanings, so let's first have an overview:

- Beat can mean a pulse in music, as in "keeping the beat", "off-beat".
- It can mean a pause or hesitation in a script, as in "I love you. (Beat) I think."
- It can mean a unit of dialogue within a scene, as in "beat sheet".

It's the last meaning we're concerned with here. A "beat" in dramatic writing comes from the teaching of Konstantin Stanislavski, the influential Russian theatre director. His teaching led directly to the Method Acting style associated with actors such as Marlon Brando and James Dean.

"Beat" just means "bit", said in a strong Russian accent. In rehearsal, Stanslavski broke down each scene into small chunks, which he called "bits" or "units". The Russian word for bit, *kusok*, is the word you'd use for "bit of cake" or "chunk of wood".

So, a beat is very practical - something almost physical that can be felt and manipulated, rather than something abstract.

In terms of scale, it's useful to think of a scene as being like a fiction chapter. A beat is a smaller unit, more like a paragraph or sentence.

Note that "beat" isn't a scientific term with a clear definition. Different directors and actors will have different ideas on analysing beats in a scene. It's quite individual. It's best to think of beats as a useful tool for breaking down a long text.

Stanislavski thought that by breaking a scene down into beats, actors could fully understand each moment. Then, they could pull the pieces all together into a coherent flow.

This systematic approach helps actors to physicalize the script, and work out how to get from one moment to the next, following a clear psychological logic.

For Stanislavski, this was as a huge improvement on previous acting technique. Before his revolutionary teaching, actors declaimed the words in a much more mannered way. Stanislavski's teaching paved the way for greater psychological logic and realism.

Breaking down beats

You may have heard of "beat sheets" used by screenwriters. They're simply Stanislavski-style breakdowns of the key dramatic actions in a scene.

Beat sheets are a tremendously helpful tool for analysing how the action of a scene develops moment by moment.

Say the main action of a scene is: Hamlet finds out who the grave belongs to. This is from *Hamlet Act V scene i* - the one with the skull.

This overarching action can be broken down further into constituent actions, eg:

- Hamlet questions the gravedigger.
- The gravedigger deflects his questions.
- Hamlet recalls past memories, and so on.

Note that "action" in this sense doesn't refer to physical movement, but to dramatic action - the underlying intention or impulse. Check out the section on *Dramatic Action* for more about this.

Subtext

The subtext is literally what's under the text. The emotional impulses hidden beneath the surface dialogue. The secret of the text, if you like.

Sometimes, the surface meaning and the subtext are the same. For example, when someone says "get lost!", with the intention of sending someone away.

More often, though, there's a gap between the surface meaning and the subtext.

For example, when someone says "get lost!", while tenderly stroking someone's cheek.

Or "I love you", while secretly drawing a knife from their pocket.

But the subtext of a line isn't always so cut and dried. Lines can be played in many different ways.

Actors exploring a script will often take a line with an apparently clear, literal meaning, and find different, more interesting ways to play it.

Even a line as simple as "get lost!" can be played with lots of different intentions and intensities.

Is it an instruction? A warning? A put-down? A dismissal?

Could it even be an expression of affection?

Say Kay pulls Jem close and murmurs "get lost!" softly in his ear. Perhaps it's a standing joke between the couple, or affection with a subtle threat beneath?

If there's a big gap between the surface meaning and subtext, it's called playing "against the line".

This awareness of beats and subtext can be really helpful in editing. I often use beats to tighten scenes, and edit more incisively.

Once I know the arc of a scene, I break it down into broad beats - a beat sheet. This gives me a sense of the emotional journey of the characters. Sometimes, I play around with the order of beats at this point.

When I edit, I often use finer beats to strengthen my dialogue. To do this, I read each line with an acting approach in mind, looking for the intention of the line.

This often reveals anything that's fuzzy or muddy, and can be cut. It's also a good way to spot whether there are too many beats in a line.

It can also reveal whether you're simply repeating the same impulse in different ways.

For example, saying "Get lost! Get the hell out of here! Move yourself!" is essentially the same impulse expressed in three different ways. In this case, I'd probably choose the strongest version and ditch the others. Less is more.

As I've gained more experience as a writer, I've tuned in more to beats, and I'm less prone to overwriting. It's one of the commonest issues with dialogue when you're starting out. Writers love words, so it's no surprise that their characters are often overwordy, too.

It's crucial also to read dialogue aloud to hear the beats. Listen out for clarity and strength of lines, endings and beginnings. Check whether the impulse is supported by the rhythm.

Even this careful editing won't give you a perfect draft. A director and actors will bring their own creativity and interpretation to your writing. They'll always make discoveries you didn't remotely dream of. Sometimes, you'll then need to tweak the script to bring out aspects of the performance.

And at some stage, your characters will no longer belong to you. They'll break free and have independent lives that will surprise and amaze you. It's a strange and wonderful feeling, and you need to let go at this point.

Beats help you to understand the bones beneath the surface of your characters - the rhythm of their drives and desires. Using beats to structure and edit your scenes will create more powerful, emotionally authentic characters. They'll express themselves through dramatic actions, not just words.

Look out, too, for the spaces between lines of dialogue. They're just as important as the lines themselves. They're like the silence in music that lets the melody shine out.

TRY THIS:
Pick a film you like and break down a scene into broad beats, to see how it's structured.

What's the overarching action of each beat? Can you identify a primary dramatic action that can be expressed as a verb? For example, to punish, to overturn, to appease.

Look at the dramatic actions for each character. Is there enough contrast between them? Do their dramatic actions escalate, or do they repeat?

Use the beat structure you've identified to write a scene of your own, in a different world, with your own characters.

TRY THIS:
Use beats to nail the intentions behind your characters' lines of dialogue. Express these as action verbs. For example: *to cajole, to hurt, to divert.*

Once you've clarified this, can you spot any repetition? Any places where the dialogue can be cut? Where the impulses are muddy?

Try changing individual words. Does this clarify or change the intention, or its intensity?

How do small nuances make a difference?

TRY THIS:
Choose a line spoken by a character, and work out the underlying impulse. Now, brainstorm 30 different ways of expressing this same impulse in dialogue.

Think about literal ways, different intensities, registers, subtext, irony, status.

What kinds of different character come to mind? How do small nuances change the nature, class, or context of the character?

TRY THIS:

Look at the ends and beginnings of lines. What do you notice?

Are they forceful, or subtle? Write a few different versions, to see the effect.

Now, mark the beats and look at the transitions between them. Do the beats merge into each other? Is there an implied space between? Or an actual space? Write some variations.

Now read your versions aloud. Listen to the rhythm of the line and spaces. What does each say about the characters?

TRY THIS:

Find some examples of lines of dialogue that seem to express more than one beat. Read aloud. What does it feel like? Where does the shift happen?

Can the lines easily be divided into beats? Are there any ambiguities? Why and when might you want ambiguity?

See also: Wants and Stakes, Stanislavski, Dramatic Action.

Further reading:

Stanislavski, C. (2013) *An Actor Prepares*. London, Bloomsbury Academic.

Wants and Stakes

There's a familiar question from the world of acting: "What's my motivation?"

With this question, the actor is asking about their character, and what's driving them through the scene.

Whether you call it motivation, drive, want, impulse, it comes from the work of Stanislavski.

He believed that characters needed to be actively propelled through a scene by a burning desire. If a character doesn't have a strong desire, then they're inherently undramatic.

It doesn't mean everyone needs to be haring around, full of action all the time.

A character's desire might be to spend all day lounging on the couch, watching TV.

This desire put them fiercely at odds with their partner, who wants them to roll up their sleeves, and go out and get a job.

A physics metaphor might be helpful here. Think of your characters as bodies propelled by energetic forces. Those forces might be like gravity, keeping them grounded and stable. Or they might be like electricity, sending a bolt through them and jumping forwards or backwards.

When these forces drive bodies together on a collision course, there's a conflict, and that's a good starting point for a scene.

If none of your characters are on a collision course, there's little scope for drama. So, you'll struggle to make them dramatically interesting.

If your characters seem flat and underpowered, it may be that they're too happy! Look at what's driving them, what's put them on a collision course, and amplify it to the point where they take off.

Even happiness can be taken to an extreme, to the point where it becomes a burning desire. Imagine a super-joyous, constantly smiling character. If they're so bent on being happy at all costs, what's going on under the surface, to drive this unusual behaviour? Unless they're the Dalai Lama, it's likely there's a festering secret to uncover.

But burning desires and "wants" also imply their opposites. The things we don't want. The things we're desperate to avoid: fear, poverty, boredom, death, rejection.

So, every want has its corresponding shadow side.

If you're desperate for a well-paid job, it implies a fear of poverty. If you're hungry for an exciting lover, it implies a fear of boredom. Wanting to look younger than you are implies a fear of ageing. If you've ever engaged with the work of the psychologist Carl Jung, you'll be familiar with this "shadow side" thinking.

These fears may not be entirely obvious on the surface, but they're worth digging into, for a sense of nuance and complexity in your characters' psychology. So, look at all your characters' burning wants, and investigate the shadow side. What are they running from, as well as toward? Can you amplify this drive?

Often, characters are at their most compelling when they have conflicting wants. Sometimes, the conflict is between inner and social values, for example, political beliefs versus family loyalty. Or, they may have competing inner instincts - a fruitful source of conflict! Maybe they're fatally attracted to their lover, but can't bear the thought of hurting their long-term partner (lust versus loyalty)? Maybe they long for exotic travels, but don't want to leave their home (excitement versus security)?

93

Finding a knotty collision of desires like this can provide a strong thematic core to drive a story.

But as well as being driven by wants and needs, people are also driven by what they don't want - what they stand to *lose*.

In other words, what's at stake if they don't get their deepest desire?

Lack of stakes is one of the most frequent reasons I see for characters and their stories falling flat. They have a burning desire, all right - getting a well-paid job, winning the competition, finding love, robbing the bank - but if they don't get what they want... nothing happens.

They think "meh" and bumble on as usual, totally unbothered by their failure to achieve their goal.

If that's the case, they'll lack drive and momentum.

You need to set things up so that your characters' failure really, really hurts.

Every want - the need to win - needs to be reinforced by corresponding stakes - what they stand to lose.

Your characters will then be propelled by both a carrot and stick - a positive and a negative.

Think of wants and stakes as twin forces which combine to keep the character on track.

So, if they don't get the well-paid job, what's at stake if they don't get it? Will they just be a bit disappointed, and carry on as before?

Or will they be thrown out of their house, because they're up to their ears in debt? Maybe the job is their last possible chance to turn things round?

If they don't win the competition and the massive prize, how will they afford the life-saving operation for their sick child?

Try to create high stakes as well as powerful wants. Then, your characters can't just back down from their want, and drain the momentum from their story. Keep up the pressure, build strong needs into their underlying psyche. You'll then find they take dramatic action under their own natural steam.

TRY THIS:
Look at scenes in your work in progress and establish the characters' wants, and the dramatic actions needed to fulfil them.

Then, for each want, identify its shadow side, and what's at stake for the characters. Once you've identified these psychological drives, explore ways for your characters to express their wants, fears and stakes through actions.

You may find that doing this exploration helps you to come up with dramatic actions more easily.

See also: Stanislavski, Maslow, Dramatic Action.

Further reading:
Caldarone, M. and Lloyd-Williams, M. (2017) *Actions: The Actors' Thesaurus*. London, Nick Hern.

Stanislavski, C. (2013) *An Actor Prepares*. London, Bloomsbury Academic.

Objects

Objects are particularly useful in dramatic writing. They help to make internal action visible, by externalizing what's going on inside characters.

For example, two characters in a marriage breakdown can show this externally, through what they throw around or break.

Sound familiar? Yes! Objects help you to show, rather than tell.

Objects between two characters can act as a point of negotiation, conflict or connection.

They can also provide a vehicle for subtext, allowing characters to express their feelings obliquely, through the object, rather than through on-the-nose dialogue.

They can be used for exposition, as in the example of a blackboard or map used to outline a campaign.

Objects can even become imbued with character themselves. They can stand in for absent characters, be puppeted, and provide solitary characters with someone to interact with, as in the Tom Hanks movie, *Cast Away*.

Above all, they add rich potential for different kinds of character interaction, by creating a physical link between them.

With any object in a scene, it's useful to brainstorm the different ways they can be used by, or impact on, your characters. Particularly on stage, every physical object needs to earn its place. It will become richer and more interestingly layered if it can be transformed, undergo a journey or have different resonances and uses, at different times in the story.

To explore this, use objects as a basis for brainstorming verbs - transitive and intransitive - and dramatic actions. Look for contrasts and opposites, and ways that characters can wrangle and be impacted by the object.

For this section, I've divided objects into different kinds. Each category can be used as an exercise or inspiration for a scene.

Immovable objects (tree, boulder, skip, house)

Some objects are on such a big scale that they're part of the scenery. They may even dominate the surroundings, and impose certain kinds of behaviour or movement on the characters.

Example: The balcony in Shakespeare's *Romeo and Juliet*.

TRY THIS:

Develop the key objects in your scene by brainstorming verbs. Look for contrasts – for example: *above/below, inside/outside, deface/clean, build/destroy*.

What do people usually do with this object? And look beyond typical uses for unusual, transgressive or symbolic actions.

Do any of these objects have territorial meaning? If they're moved to a different place, do they lose their power? For example, something on a pedestal in an art gallery might appear quite ordinary when it's in the back of a van. Do the objects have any taboos or boundaries that can be honoured or breached? Maybe they're imbued with supernatural powers?

Once you've brainstormed verbs and dramatic actions, try placing them in different sequences. For example: Find, build, topple. Lose, find. Use index cards to rearrange the actions, if you like.

Imagine your sequence as a silent scene. Does it have story potential? Does it develop, change or escalate?

Movable objects (table, car, throne)

At this scale, objects are big enough to act as obstacles. They can be clambered on, and it might take more than one person to shift them.

At this scale, they may have literal or symbolic value, or both. They may demand respect, and not always get it.

Movable objects at this scale have typical uses. But what about untypical use? Brainstorm unexpected, transgressive and disruptive uses of the objects in your scene.

As an extreme (and fun) example, check out the films of Jackie Chan. He's well known for his inventive use of objects in iconic fight scenes.

Another example is *The Piano* (1993), directed by Jane Campion.

TRY THIS:
Explore the visual potential of objects in your script.

Think of how they might look in a movie. Imagine your characters interacting with the objects in different ways – for example, under a car or table, or standing behind a throne. What does this do to the dynamics and status of your characters?

Imagine these objects transformed in different ways - *painted, upturned, covered, taken hostage*. What characters and stories come to mind? What's the visual impact?

Try *before/after* scenarios. For example, a muddy car is cleaned, or a valuable table scratched. This can be a good way to create bookends for a scene arc.

Try the effect of moving these objects to a different, contrasting place. How does their meaning and impact change?

Portable objects (guitar, vase, fishing rod)

Objects like these that are easy to carry around are likely to be personal rather than social possessions. They may come with a strong sense of ownership and pride, even identity.

Objects at this scale lend themselves to transfer between characters. They can be willingly exchanged, unwillingly yielded, stolen or hidden.

They can sometimes be invested with high value, whether financial or emotional. This makes their transfer between characters fraught with meaning.

Example: The guitar in *El Mariachi* (1992), directed by Robert Rodriguez.

> **TRY THIS:**
> Imagine an object of this size for your character. Imagine it old, then imagine it new. What different stories are suggested?
>
> How can you make the object important? Raise the stakes. For example, imagine the object gone. What does that mean for the character?
>
> Are there any limits to this object's portability? Are there situations where it would be very unlikely to appear, or might be kept hidden? See how you can use this to create contrast.

Living objects (dog, hen, snake)

Animals and other beasts aren't objects, of course. However, they're still invested with some of the qualities of objects – for example, ownership, value and portability.

They're also a strong presence in any scene, and can provide a foil for your characters to engage with and speak to. If your character needs to reveal their inner life, one way to dramatize this is to give them a "companion animal" for interaction.

Some animals are safe, familiar and domestic - budgies, cats, dogs. Others are exotic and might be threatening. *Snakes on a Plane*, anyone?

Just as with human characters, there's a danger of imbuing animals with stereotypes. But animals are alive and unpredictable. Try turning expectations on their heads to create surprise and tension. Remember the killer rabbit in *Monty Python and the Holy Grail*?

One of the features of human-animal interaction is degree of control. Who's in charge of whom?

Example: Elgar the cat in in the BBC Radio 4 comedy series, *Ed Reardon's Week*.

99

TRY THIS:
Explore the presence of different animals in your scene. How does the presence of animals alter the dynamics?

Imagine different sizes and kinds of animal. How does this change your characters and their dramatic potential?

Explore the status of an animal in the scene. Can you include a status shift? Why and how might the power relationship change?

Brainstorm animal verbs: tame, trap, feed, heal, and the use of significant objects and transformations involving animals.

Objects as character (doll, mask, volleyball)

Objects may not be alive. But they can still be imbued with life, or animated. Sometimes objects can take on enough life to become practically a character in their own right.

Dolls and puppets naturally lend themselves to this treatment, but many other objects can be animated, too. Clothes are very often used for animation in theatre, and can easily create an additional character presence on stage.

Animating an object also gives your human characters another presence to engage with in the scene.

The object doesn't need literally to speak. It might just be a foil for the character's monologue, giving it focus and allowing the actor to be more expressive.

This technique is also used in psychodrama, a form of psychotherapy where objects are used to externalize emotions. You might, for example, talk to a chair as though it were a person from your past, to help you articulate your feelings and get them outside yourself.

In terms of dialogue, using an object as a character can also be a vivid way to reveal exposition, or a character's inner life. Characters are sometimes seen talking to mirrors, or using a hairbrush as a microphone.

Example: Wilson the volleyball in the Tom Hanks film *Cast Away*.

100

TRY THIS:

Do you have any scenes where your characters are alone?

Explore the potential of objects in the scene. Can any be used as a vehicle for expression? What happens when your character speaks to the object?

Now, imagine the object speaking. What would it say? Write it into a "dialogue" scene with your character. Then try removing the object's side of the dialogue. Does it work when its contribution is implied, but not heard?

Now, try the effect of objects-as-characters in a scene with more than one performer. For example, two children with a doll or chair.

Small objects (ring, key, pebble)

Objects at a scale smaller than hand-size have different possibilities.

They can be hidden, thrown, swallowed, planted, made to disappear.

Depending on your medium, they may not have a big visual impact. A ring, for example, can be a potent object in a film close-up, but not in a wide landscape shot.

Small objects may be extremely valuable and high status. They may be fragile.

They can be easily transferred, broken or stolen, making them extra vulnerable.

They may be a crucial component in a larger structure, such as a missing screw or spark plug. So, even if they're tiny, they can still have a huge dramatic impact.

Example: The ring in *Lord of the Rings*.

TRY THIS:

Explore the use of small objects in your scene. Identify their physical properties: weight, colour, material. What can they be used for, apart from their normal use?

What happens if you multiply the number of objects? Do they become more or less valuable? Is there a point where a lot of these small objects become a nuisance? For example, a single marble, compared with a big box of marbles.

How valuable is the object? Does it have the same value to every character in your story, or does it vary? What happens when you change this? For example, a child's sketch may be valuable to the child's parents, but not to a family visitor.

What's the value system around objects in your script? For example, ice skates or skater dresses might be valuable, and high fashion not. Or the other way round!

What happens if you move the goalposts – either putting the valuable object in the wrong context, or putting something low-value into its right context. For example, a broken necklace in a junk shop is found by a leading collector of vintage jewellery. How does the value and meaning of the object change?

Explore the transfer of the objects between characters and places. How can they be transferred? In person? By post? How easy is this, and how long does it take? What happens if you make transfer easy, and more difficult?

Wearable objects

Clothes, hats and shoes are extremely powerful creators of character. If you haven't played with a dressing-up box since childhood, now's the time!

What your characters wear has a huge impact on how they move and feel, so take your time to consider this carefully. If you can, try on the type of clothes they'd wear. Vintage clothes in second-hand shops are a great source of inspiration. Older garments often have different qualities. They're weightier, and more rigid. Often, the fabric is thicker and made to last.

In period dramas, actors will wear significant costume items in rehearsal. Women's clothes at different periods has been incredibly restrictive. To embody these characters successfully, it's vital to understand how they felt physically, at the most basic level. So, even if actors can't wear a full costume to rehearse, they'll wear improvised shaping, such as a mock crinoline, or bustle padding.

Even with modern dramas, actors will often find the right kind of footwear to rehearse in early on, as this affects their character's movements, posture and demeanour so much. High heels, flat heels, springy trainers or bare feet - they all evoke different characters and identities, and lead to different kinds of behaviour.

Wigs and hats - their presence and absence - are important for appearance and self-identity. They can also be important indicators of social status and freedoms.

Sometimes, a well-chosen wearable can become a character emblem and shorthand. It can take on semiotic significance, and become a sign or symbol of the character in its own right. An example is Indiana Jones' iconic fedora hat.

Could you use this idea with your own protagonist, to amplify their impact? What's unique about them that could be epitomized through their clothes or possessions? If you saw them only in silhouette, would they be recognisable?

Example: The costumes in any movie version of *Pride and Prejudice*.

TRY THIS:

Consider how clothes can be used to transform characters in your scene. Are they used as a disguise or mask? Or for another kind of transformation, such as status, wealth or confidence?

Explore the physical properties of their clothes: weight, colour, material. Brainstorm ways that they can be worn, and also uses beyond wearing. Signalling? Ripped up for bandages? Knotted to join two things together?

Brainstorm dramatic actions using items of clothing - *rip, reveal, conceal, muddy, wash, threaten*. How might you expand or escalate the use of clothes in your scene?

Consider the freedom and restriction of your characters' clothes. How do they make characters move in different terrains and territories?

Are the clothes heavy, restrictive, liberating, loud, sedate, young, old, familiar, exotic? How might these qualities change your actions? Brainstorm some verbs, and their opposites. Try using this pair of verbs to create a scene arc.

TRY THIS:

Go to a second-hand or theatrical costume shop and try on costumes.

Take notes on how you feel, in terms of movement, energy and status.

Note textures and material qualities and whether they're comfortable, uncomfortable, plain, printed, embellished, stretchy, hand or machine-finished.

Consider the life of the clothes, and what difference it would make if they were brand new, a gift, a legacy. Who made them? Would your character be aware of the maker?

Try loud clothes and quieter ones. Where might you go wearing these clothes, to fit in, or to disrupt?

Think about which of the clothes feel like an invitation to behave differently.

See also: Dramatic Action, Transformation, Physicality, Status, Improv.

Physicality

The word "drama" comes from the ancient Greek word *dran*, meaning "to do, act".

Action is right at the heart of dramatic writing.

And not just any kind of action. Physical action that can be done, and seen.

In scripts, inert characters who don't do much aren't interesting. To be honest, they're not that interesting in fiction, either.

Characters might be thinking amazing thoughts, and internally reaching a crucial turning-point in their lives. But in drama, we won't know this, unless

- they take physical action that we can see, or
- you allow them to voice their thoughts, as in voiceover or soliloquy.

In drama, voiceover and soliloquy are distinct techniques for conveying interior (mental) spaces. They need careful handling and shouldn't be used lightly - say, as an easy way to drop in exposition. Like flashbacks, they're sometimes considered an expositional cop-out, so it's best to treat them with the respect and suspicion they deserve. There's more about this in the sections on *Space* and *Time*.

So, the dominant mode of dramatic technique is external physical action, doing and showing.

However, physical action isn't all big gestures and action hero stuff. It comes in different flavours. So, it's useful to break it down into different kinds.

Before moving on, I'll assume you're familiar with the sections on *Dramatic Action, Wants and Stakes* and *Show and Tell*. They lay the foundations for thinking about action and its role in scriptwriting.

This section looks at different kinds of physical actions, to suggest ways of developing your scenes.

Bold actions (chop, run, upturn, feed)

Big, bold expressive actions are often seen in action films, and at critical moments of drama. Big movement, change, speed, incisiveness jolt the audience, by disrupting the normal pace and intensity of everyday behaviour. Actions like this can signal a significant moment in the story.

But that's not all there is to physicality in dramatic writing. For one thing, if your characters only ever perform high-intensity actions such as fighting and chasing, they'll get boring. It sounds paradoxical - more action means more excitement, right? But stories need light and shade, action and rest, to refresh the audience's palate.

Too much full-on action is like scoffing too much over-rich chocolate fudge. It starts out great, then the senses get dulled, and it gets a bit samey. It's amazing how quickly we can get habituated to something, and start looking out for the next novelty.

So, with bold actions, you need to use them carefully, and consider clarity and context.

In drama, intentional action is sometimes called "gesture". In this context, it doesn't mean spontaneous gesticulation, as in using your hands expressively. It refers to powerful, clear movements with a dramatic impulse behind them.

In this sense, bold actions can include gestures such as anoint, feed, give and take, just as much as leap or smash.

Bold physical actions can have different underlying emotions and impulses. Sometimes, it's an impulse to destroy (chop, smash).

106

Sometimes it's an impulse away from something (flee, push). Sometimes it's an impulse towards (chase, hunt), or an impulse to restore or give (sweep, present).

If your character has reached a key turning-point, can they express it through a bold physical action?

Rather than having your character talk about their feelings, brainstorm how they might externalize those emotions in a physical, visible way.

You can also develop action further by thinking about subtext. External actions can sometimes contradict what's going on inside the characters. Appearances can be deceptive. For example, as an act of love, a character might destroy some love letters. Or they might lovingly seduce another character, as an act of manipulation.

Writing physical action with a contradictory subtext is a powerful way to create tension. Often, this can be done by setting up the context, so that the audience is primed. In other words, use dramatic irony. For example, in the movie and stage play *Dangerous Liaisons*, the writer Christopher Hampton lets the audience know that the plotters want to seduce the innocent Cecile. So, when we see a seduction scene with romantic gestures, we also see the deceitful subtext.

Occasionally, words themselves can be gestures. For example, words can be used to name, anoint, banish, marry, baptise. This usage is mostly seen in ritual or ceremonial situations. "I now declare you man and wife" is a gesture conveyed through an act of speech.

But you can also use this technique in more subtle situations. Naming and use of names, for example, can be a powerful gesture. Your character might be acknowledging their estranged, long-lost mother, by calling them "mother" for the first time. Or use someone's childhood nickname instead of their formal workplace name. Naming or renaming can be used as a kind of anointment, to establish intimacy, or to demean. It can be extraordinarily potent in the right context.

TRY THIS:

Choose something in the world of your script - a possession, prop or piece of furniture.

Brainstorm verbs that can be done with your chosen object - as many as possible.

Think of large and small gestures, destructive and nurturing, fast and slow.

Then read back your list. Does anything surprise you? Shock you? Move you in any way?

Write this action into your scene.

Unusual actions (gut fish, play ice-hockey, mend shirt, build hut)

Actions that are everyday to you might be unusual to many people! What's unusual depends on context. An everyday activity for you might be highly intriguing for others.

For example, in recent years, Norway has had international TV hits with its "slow TV" footage of sleigh rides, log fires and knitting. Their snowy way of life is fascinating for people used to warmer climates. The Australians followed suit with *The Ghan*, showing an epic train journey across the central Australian desert. Although very little drama happened, the detail of these distinctive worlds and activities captured many people's imaginations.

Might some of the ordinary things you do be more intriguing than you think? Do you have any unusual expertise or do activities that could be exploited in a story? What aspects of your job take you into places normally hidden from view?

People in the world of arts and literature are surprisingly similar in social background. The lack of diversity and social mobility in the UK arts, for example, was starkly revealed in a 2018 survey by Goldsmiths University. It showed that people in the arts might think of themselves as diverse and wide-open to new experiences. But in practice, they're socially limited.

So, your experience of work - whether as an electrician, butcher, gardener or cubicle worker - is likely to be a rich seam of processes and activities to plunder.

Look out, in particular, for anything physical that may be unusual to others. When I do copywriting jobs for small companies, I'm fascinated by the work they do on a daily basis. Their everyday life includes diving, hauling up floorboards, and setting up lighting rigs. Some of my friends have intriguing hobbies, too, including longbow archery and beekeeping.

Look at your work and skills, and those of your friends, and see if any of them can be used for your characters. Even if their actions aren't big and bold, they might be visually intriguing and be interesting in a scene.

Or, if the activity isn't inherently dynamic, try creating subtext and tension, by setting it in an incongruent place. For example, gutting a fish in a bathroom, or sewing at an ice-hockey match. Or try using incongruent dialogue, as in Tarantino's *Pulp Fiction*, and the famous hamburger-eating scene against a background of murder.

If your scene lacks visual interest or the dialogue is too expositional, try using physical actions to create an intriguing juxtaposition. Give the characters something to play against.

Interior actions (think, ponder, wonder, fear)

If you're used to writing fiction, it's easy to think of interior action as dramatic. After all, your characters may be wrestling internally with life-and-death matters, seismic revelations, and desperate fears.

And one of the great advantages of fiction technique is the ability to climb right inside characters' heads, and see their inner workings. The internal viewpoints of fiction, including first person and free indirect style, allow writers to convey characters' rich interior lives very effectively.

But this interior life doesn't translate well to the visual, external world of dramatic writing.

Even if your character is thinking deep and hard, all we'll see is tense face muscles, and maybe some sweat, which can be read as pretty well anything. A character thinking might just about work in a movie close-up, but will hardly register at all in a wide shot, or on stage.

If interior action is going to be shown, it needs to be dramatized - translated into visible dramatic action.

I see a lot of writing in progress which is overly reliant on characters' interior lives, and lacks pace and immediacy. It can be hard to identify exactly what's missing. But it's easy to spot, once you're familiar with the rigours of dramatic technique.

For example, dramatic thinking lets you more easily see that the characters are just sitting in a café and talking about the past, or standing at a bus stop waiting for something to happen. They might be somewhere unusual and exciting (say, at the races), but if they're just talking about someone else, it's not dramatic. The screenwriter and playwright David Mamet has put this more bluntly: "Two characters talking about a third is a crock of shit."

It's easy to highlight structural inertia like this in fiction, by using storyboarding. Storyboards are a sequence of sketches showing what happens in a camera shot or sequence. You don't need good drawing skills to do this. Rough stick people are fine.

Drawing a storyboard sketch can help you to capture the main essence of a scene. It'll show you whether your characters are active or static and sitting around. You'll probably need a mix, as too much of any one thing gets boring.

With your scene sketch, ask yourself if it's clear what's going on. Would it be clear to someone who didn't speak your language? Is anyone just talking, reminiscing, or thinking about their inner pain or joy? Can you translate this interior life into externalized drama?

Once you've done all you can to dramatize your scenes, there will still be moments when your characters want to reflect or think. But often, you can make this less obvious with a few simple line edits.

First, look out for verbs of interior action - *think, imagine, worry, reflect*, etc. They can often be deleted, leaving just the thoughts themselves. For example:

> *Jed headed for the bar. "Damn," he thought.*
> *"They've rung last orders. Maybe it's too late?"*

This can be rendered in free indirect style as:

> *Jed headed for the bar. Damn. They'd rung last*
> *orders. Maybe it was too late?*

Using fewer "thought" words can put readers right inside the character's head. It's emotionally closer, and the reading experience can be more immersive.

Then, you can often delete sensory verbs – for example: *see, taste, smell, hear, touch.*

> *She stopped. She could hear the jackdaws all*
> *around, cawing as they came into roost.*

can become

> *She stopped. The jackdaws were cawing all*
> *around as they came into roost.*

If you take away that extra verb, hear, the viewpoint is still clear.

Verbs of perception and the senses are an extra narrative frame that you don't really need. By cutting them, you can bring readers closer to the characters.

TRY THIS:

Use storyboarding to sketch what's going on in your fiction scenes. Do this really quickly - no more than 30 seconds for each one. You're just trying to grab the essence.

What do you discover about the main action of your scenes? Are they physical and visible, static or internal? Are they similar, or do you have a good mix of action, reflection and dialogue? Can any scenes be made livelier by moving them to a more visually interesting or active setting?

Looking at your sketches, are all the characters truly needed, and pulling their weight? What happens if you remove one of them? Can anyone be brought into the scene at a later stage, to step things up and vary the interaction?

Physical force fields

I sometimes think of my characters as physical force fields, with drives, wants, and a physical nature. They collide in the world, take up space, energise and deplete each other, and interact in different ways.

It's a useful metaphor, because when you're deeply entangled in characters' inner lives and voices, it can be hard to see the bigger picture of their outward actions.

Storyboarding can help, but for me, it lacks the dimension of movement. So, to develop your scenes further, you might want to explore different ways to animate your characters.

Try imagining your scene without any dialogue at all, as a silent movie. How does it read? Could someone who doesn't speak your language work out what the scene is about?

Or try using objects such as children's toys, and plot their movements on the table. You can even use different kinds of fruit for this. Imagine an army of grapes surrounding a large baking apple. It sounds odd, but it can give a good sense of the physical entities, their interrelation, and their relationship to the setting. For example, two small characters in a cavernous empty space interact very differently to five large characters crammed into a small one.

Try looking at your characters in this bold, almost graphic way, as physical forces. Can you see differences between them in status, or power? How might you amp up these differences, to create greater tension?

What's the broad sweep of movement or transformation in your scene? For example, do your characters transition from

112

confinement to escape? From peace to upheaval? From defeated to victorious?

If you visualize the physicality of your scene and character relationships, you'll be able to see how they "read" dramatically, without the distraction of words.

TRY THIS:

Brainstorm ways your character might express different emotions, such as rage, joy, boredom.

When you've exhausted the usual ways, have them look around at their environment and see how they might use anything they find to express these emotions. For example, objects, furniture, animals, people. Be as inventive as you can.

Does anything jump out at you as fresh and intriguing? Does it make a difference whether the gesture is slow or fast? Deliberate or spontaneous? Does it make a difference whether anyone else is in the room, and their status in relation to your character?

What actions would your character absolutely never do, and why?

Write one of these actions into your scene.

See also: Dramatic Action, Show and Tell, Wants and Stakes, Space, Objects, Transformation.

Contrast

Contrast is an important tool for writers, because it creates difference, and difference creates tension.

Tension, in turn, creates dynamic flow and momentum. This keeps your reader engaged.

Imagine a scene of interaction between two characters of a similar class, age, appearance, status and values.

They're talking about their neighbours, say, and their annoying habit of playing loud music at three in the morning.

Even though they're irritated and uptight about the subject, they're not really in tension.

Dramatically speaking, they're too similar. They're on the same page. They want and value the same things. Despite the irritation, they're friendly and collaborative in conversation.

And the problem is, this is deadly dull for readers.

It might be interesting to briefly eavesdrop on these characters, but unless there's change and disruption between them, the action won't take off.

Ordinary conversation is rarely dramatic, as it doesn't have the underlying engine of dramatic tension built in.

To create scope for tension and change, create strong contrast between your characters.

It'll make your scenes easier to write, and interest your readers more, because interaction between contrasting characters is less predictable.

So, where can you build in contrast?

Amp up your antagonist

At a very basic level, do you have a strong antagonist?

Writers are often so invested in the life of their protagonist that they forget to create a fully-fledged, powerful antagonist.

They create a lead character with terrible personal demons or troubled circumstances. Someone who's really up against it, fighting big battles.

But then they give them supportive friends, not enemies.

This makes it pretty well impossible to write dynamic, dramatic scenes. It often leads to solo stories that are internalized and abstract. Stories where characters reflect on their woes, and think about the past, and how they got to this point. Where they spend lonely hours doing up cottages, learning to run marathons, planning a future, and other transformative and worthy but ultimately solo and inward activities.

A solid protagonist-antagonist relationship gives you far greater scope for active, tension-filled scenes.

Scenes where they clash, fight and undermine each other. Where friendly appearances belie a subtext of jealousy and manipulation. Where secrets create distrust and shifting allegiances. Where they launch bombs of revelation into each other's midst. Where they turn up on a mission at the worst possible times in each other's lives.

That's the stuff of drama!

However, when you're creating your antagonist, be sure not to create one who is simply a foil for the protagonist.

Yes, they'll be thematically linked, and manifest conflicting values. But they need to be a real character with their own strong life, wants and hinterland.

115

Put them in a high-stakes setting together, and let the fur fly!

And imagine your protagonists, antagonists and all secondary characters being played by actors. An actor won't thank you for an underrealized character who is little more than a cipher or device. Cast your characters in your head, even the walk-ons with only a few lines to say. This will help you treat them as individuals, not just plot devices.

Give them interesting and memorable lines. Imagine their backstory, and what life they go back to, once they've crossed paths with your lead characters. Maybe you'll discover they've a lot to say!

Subtext

Subtext is a contrasting meaning hidden below the surface words. For example, imagine three sisters:

> **Text:** *Dad, you're amazing and I love you to bits.*
> **Subtext:** *Give me a third of your kingdom*

This is from King Lear.

Or imagine a salesman asking for a better job:

> **Text:** *Hey boss, give me a job at HQ!*
> **Subtext:** *I'm shattered and on my knees. Plus you owe me one.*

This is from *Death of a Salesman*.

One of the ways that actors make dialogue more interesting is by exploring subtext. It's a form of contrast between the surface and what lies beneath. It creates all-important dramatic tension.

Sometimes, dialogue does what's on the tin, and is aligned clearly with its actions. For example:

116

Pointing to the exit: *Get lost!*
Planting a kiss: *I love you.*
Indicating the gold ring/ bag of tomatoes:
How much?

But in these examples, there's no tension between the surface of the line, and the underlying intention. Actors can often rescue boring dialogue by playing "against the line". Essentially, they find a contrary subtext.

For example:

Undressing seductively: *Get lost!*
Pouring poison into the goblet: *I love you.*
Examining fingernails: *How much?*

How can you use this knowledge? In two main ways:

Firstly, pair your dialogue with a subtextual action, to create an ironic contrast.

Secondly, write more oblique, less on-the-nose dialogue that contrasts with the subtext of the scene.

Whichever you choose, think of the actor delivering your lines, and imbue them with plenty of interest.

TRY THIS:

Choose a scene from your writing and analyze the dialogue. Is it on the nose? Does its intention align squarely with the words?

If so, create tension by changing the subtext. One way is to give characters an activity at odds with the dialogue. For example, as in Tarantino's "hamburger" scene in *Pulp Fiction*, against a murder backdrop.

Or, prime the scene with a burning issue, then have them talk about something else. Then there's an elephant in the room, creating tension.

A classic example is Hamlet's chat with the clown gravedigger, against the backdrop of Ophelia's impending funeral. Or, the bawdy porter in Macbeth, opening the gates of "hell" while emptying his bladder.

If you can't find a way to build in dramatic contrast structurally, imagine how an actor might play "against the line". Use this contrast to create a richer subtext for your characters.

Protagonist, antagonist, momentum

A strong contrast between protagonist and antagonist gives a clearer story dynamic.

In most fiction, this dynamic forms the very spine of the story. The relationship between protagonist and antagonist crystalizes the themes of the book. Their conflict is usually about the core value at stake: justice, peace, love, freedom.

It follows, then, that the antagonist needs to appear early on in your story.

Don't wait till the mid-point, or climactic final scene, for a showdown with the antagonist.

Introduce him or her close to the start of your story - maybe just after you've established the status quo.

The antagonist typically brings an element of disruption, and often embodies the inciting incident that really kicks off your story.

If you're novel is struggling to get going, maybe you've spent too long on setup.

Try ruthless editing. Set up the protagonist's world and the status quo with a few broad strokes, then bring on the disruptive antagonist. The strong contrast between them will add an instant jolt of momentum, and get your story properly started.

Antagonists aside, minor characters, too, can be boosted by using contrast.

People have a vast mix of traits and dynamics, but writers sometimes have a limited repertoire. It might be because we don't have wide social experience. Or we don't trust ourselves to create convincing characters who are very different to us.

But characters need a wide mix, and scriptwriters have to be able to do this, because drama demands it.

Dramatists explore a theme through a range of contrasting characters who are distinct enough to reveal its different facets. These multiple viewpoints allow them to explore the theme with great complexity and richness.

So, strong contrasts need to be built in from the start.

The most crucial aspect of character contrast is what they want. If two characters want the same thing, they're not in conflict, so your scene or story will lack momentum. This is a surprisingly common reason why scenes between two people can feel flat.

In each scene, look closely at the dramatic function of each character. Sometimes, their function is too similar, and one of the characters isn't truly earning their keep, dramatically speaking.

Think of the cost of production, even if it's a novel. It'll help you decide whether the characters are pulling their weight. You might find that you can delete one, or conflate two characters into one.

For example, let's say your heroine has two frenemies who subtly bring her down. If their dramatic function is to be antagonists, so that she can overcome them and grow, then it's highly possible you don't need both characters.

In fact, two characters with a similar dramatic function can actually dilute their own impact. That's because they both need air-time, and two means less time for intense interaction between the protagonist and antagonist.

If you can't find a good reason to keep both, then it might be best to thin them out. Or, find a journey for Frenemy 2 which makes them different to Frenemy 1, such as the capacity for change or empathy.

Once you're sure each character is earning their keep dramatically, with a strong and contrasting drive and journey, dig deep into character variables.

Powerful variables with an important bearing on tension and dynamics include status, age, class, register, appearance, values, ethnicity and culture.

Beyond this are surface foibles and traits, including habits, interests, quirks, clothes, favourite food and bands, and anything to do with individuality and preference.

See where you can drive the characters further apart, giving them greater tension to work with, and you a bigger palette to draw on.

So, for example, you might have a gang of bank robbers, or whale hunters. Each gang member has different motivations, whether money, revenge, excitement, or proving themselves to their village, family, or sworn enemy.

These motivations are linked to their different values - money, justice, status, and so on.

Even within a gang of crooks, they'll have different ethics. To kill or not to kill? To leave their injured comrade behind, or not?

They'll have a range of physiques, appearances and ages, too, giving you different story options. Maybe there's a skinny young crook who can wriggle through tight spaces? Or a crook who speaks Arabic and can pass as an international banker?

These contrasts also show in characters' speech, influencing their register, vocabulary, style, and intensity. This can help you write more distinctive characters, far from the limiting grooves of your usual writing voice.

Contrast and setting

Contrast can also be used to give settings more impact. Consider your setting or world, and what might be disruptive there.

The status quo might be a quiet, safe world. Strong contrast in that world might be noise, or chaos.

For example, a peaceful library visited by workmen with pneumatic drills.

But this technique can also work the other way round. Imagine a status quo that is violent or criminal. What would disrupt that status quo the most? The opposite. Someone gentle or conformist.

For example, a bunch of mobsters shaken up by the arrival of a nun, or an accountant.

Extreme contrasts like this can be comedic, whereas more subtle contrasts can provide dramatic tension and character complexity.

It's also possible to create scenes with greater impact by setting them in a contrasting environment. For example, a love scene in a butcher's, or a huge fight in a Buddhist retreat.

The Harrison Ford film *Witness*, set in an Amish community, is a great example of exploiting the contrast between setting and action.

See also: Tension, Dramatic Action, Transformation.

Fatal Flaw

In Greek tragedy, characters were seen as being driven by a flaw or error *(hamartia)*. This fatal flaw triggered an unfortunate chain of events.

Once triggered, the tragedy would unfold under inevitable momentum, until the hero or heroine met their violent end.

The idea of "spoiler alert" would be lost on a Greek theatre-going audience. Often, they'd be familiar with the stories already.

It's thought that the ancient Greek word *hamartia* means something like "to err" or "to miss the target". So it's possible the Greeks saw their heroes as people who had lost their way, rather than being morally flawed. This ties in with their belief in destiny. They thought that individuals didn't have much personal agency, and couldn't outrun what fate had in store for them.

However, this idea has come down to us in modern storytelling as the "fatal flaw" - an expression which implies moral judgment.

It suggests that the characters are responsible for their own miserable ends, due to their tragic inadequacy. It implies that the rest of us can watch and learn. So, there's a kind of didactic or moral element involved.

Fairy tales are also thought to be morality tales, or cautionary tales to teach children about the dangers of life. Don't eat strange sweets, and don't go off with hairy strangers.

In movies, fatal flaws are more usually personal qualities such as arrogance, dishonesty, meanness or naivety. Although character traits are complex and multi-layered, taking one trait to an extreme can drive a story.

The French dramatist Molière uses this to great effect in his comedy plays, with characters who embody extreme cynicism (*The Misanthrope*) or penny-pinching (*The Miser*). He shows the terrible and hilarious repercussions of someone who refuses to address their fatal flaw.

As a film example, Mr Bean is a character based on extraordinary stupidity and naivety.

In comedy, characters typically haven't changed at all by the end. In sitcoms, for example, the characters go on a journey in each episode, but the status quo always returns at the end.

In tragedy, the characters also have a fatal flaw. But unlike comic characters, they're driven by it towards tragic consequences.

For example, Shakespeare's Hamlet suffers from the fatal flaw of indecision, and ends up being poisoned.

Othello suffers from the fatal flaw of jealousy, and ends up killing himself.

In drama, the characters learn from their flaw, and eventually turn things round. Their overall journey is one of redemption.

Take, for example, the character of Scrooge in Charles Dickens' *A Christmas Carol*.

His fatal flaw is miserliness. The three Christmas ghosts take him on a gruelling journey. At the end, he emerges shaken and changed, ready to embark on a new phase of life, a bit like a butterfly emerging from a chrysalis.

This is the shape of the "hero's journey" familiar from screenwriting. The hero's journey story template by Christopher Vogler was inspired by the work of the mythologist, Joseph Campbell. He, in turn, was inspired by the work of the psychologist, Carl Jung.

In the hero's journey model, the protagonist is driven by their fatal flaw into an unknown world to battle their demons, and come out the other side transformed.

Underlying this model is a sense of experience and learning - a personal growth trajectory. It's an individualistic model focused on personal agency.

With this kind of story, particularly in the West, audiences tend to identify with the characters and the implied morality. Whether the cautionary tragedy or the redemptive "hero's journey" drama, stories can inspire us to change.

But stories don't have to have an implied morality.

In many cultures, including ancient Greece, a fatalistic "you're doomed, whatever you do" is more usual. Sometimes, it's because the values at stake aren't personal development. They might be honour, for example, or the survival of the tribe over the individual.

It can be a shock to see a Chinese film such as *Crouching Tiger, Hidden Dragon*, where the heroine throws herself off a cliff after years of triumphant combat. We're so used to seeing great individual effort rewarded, and a sense of fair play where heroism wins through and has meaning. Throwing it away in an act of extraordinary self-denial can seem nihilistic, or disappointing.

But Western stories, too, are turning away from the "hero's journey", with its clear moral undertow.

The films of Lars von Trier, for example (*Breaking the Waves, Dancer in the Dark*) often show a naive victim character terribly oppressed, heading inexorably through a downward trajectory, towards a tragic end. His characters don't learn from their fatal flaw, seize personal agency and avoid the pitfalls.

In von Trier's films, the lack of redemption arc can make the story feel pointless. But maybe this is a more accurate reflection of real-life stories, where effort doesn't necessarily earn fair treatment, and caution doesn't necessarily protect?

In a world where bigger forces seem to hold sway over individuals, whether fate, political ideology, or capitalism, maybe these stories are cautionary and realistic?

Stories nowadays are becoming morally far more complex, with shifting allegiances and morally ambiguous characters. *Game of Thrones* is a great example of shifting moralities and a world where the characters can't trust anyone.

So, while the fatal flaw is useful for creating dramatic story arcs and journeys for your characters, be aware that not every writer or culture prefers this storytelling strategy.

See also: Dara Marks, Catharsis.

Further reading:
Dancyger, K. and Rush, J. (2002) *Alternative Scriptwriting. Successfully Breaking the Rules*. London, Routledge.

Status

Status is about power levels between characters.

When changes happen in your story, it can topple the prevailing status, and create different power dynamics between characters.

This will create tension and momentum.

So, status play is a wonderfully powerful tool for dramatic writers.

Status is easy to understand when you look at the psychology of social groups.

People are mammals, just like chimpanzees. At a deep instinctive level, we're all about pecking orders. Everyone has to find their place, whether as a socially dominant alpha male or female, or as a more submissive and retiring member of the group.

When someone challenges the social order, it creates chaos and disruption, which is an important driver in drama.

There's usually a tussle until a new order is established. Things settle down for a while, and then the next challenger comes along.

Another helpful image for status shifts comes from the world of physics. Characters are like physical bodies full of energy that are constantly in motion, colliding with each other and shifting around.

Their energy has to go somewhere, or be transformed into something else. So a character with a strong energy who wants something very strongly is bound to cause disruption in the status quo.

At story level, it's possible to think of characters in this broad way, as forces colliding, joining, and interacting in different ways.

126

What's important is that they're in constant motion, driving each other on, action leading to reaction, in an unstoppable chain.

The TV series *Game of Thrones* is a great example of this perpetual motion of shifting allegiances and dominations, as character fortunes rise and fall.

Sources of status

Depending on the group, culture and community in your story, status can be attached to different values. This is usually linked to the underlying themes of your story.

For example, some groups value political power, while others value wealth.

A group of musicians might attach status to musical prowess, while a gang of thieves might admire cunning and trickery.

Status can also be dynastic and attached to family - the elder in a tribe, or the matriarch in a mafia family.

Or it can be dependent on your job status and role in the workplace hierarchy.

Status can also be linked to morality and qualities such as honour, peacefulness and virginity, or to their opposites: delinquency, belligerence and depravity. It all depends on the culture of the group.

In some groups, youth is prized, in others, age and experience.

Note that group cultures automatically create insiders and outsiders. Outsiders may refuse to play the same status games, with interesting results.

For example, say a politician who is used to high status at work meets a group of anarchist activists. They're unlikely to be impressed by his credentials, and certainly won't show it.

A similar culture and status clash will happen when an anarchist activist enters a government building. They won't play by the normal rules of deferring to high-status government ministers.

But the anarchist collective will still have its own pecking order and status play within the group. It might depend on how long they've been a member, what marches they've been on, what anti-establishment action they've been part of. Or, if they're new and young, they might derive status from having a parent who is a well-known activist leader.

Status is at work in every area of life, in large groups and small. How can you put this to work to create more tension in your writing?

Status shift and scale

Status shifts happen at different scales.

At story scale, you might see one character rise or fall over the entire arc. For example, the tragic downfalls of King Lear and Othello. Or the rise of Forrest Gump.

Status can also rise or fall over the course of a scene.

For example, a downtrodden employee comes into the office. The boss gives them a dressing-down. However, the employee has something up their sleeve. They've won the lottery, or they've been sleeping with the boss's partner, or been promoted over the boss's head.

At the right moment, the employee lets loose this information bomb. Suddenly, the status is reversed. The boss is wrong-footed, and the employee has the upper hand.

"Underdog turns the tables" is a good example of a complete status reversal. However, a status shift needn't be so extreme.

It could be as simple as a new arrival in the scene.

Remember the pecking order! A new arrival changes the dynamics instantly. The other characters will need to adjust to the subtle rearrangement of power and priorities.

When you're introducing a new character into a scene, bear this in mind, and don't do it lightly. Any new arrival really changes the temperature, so make them count.

And rather than introducing several new characters in a oner, try introducing them one by one. That way, each one really counts and has time to make their impact.

Subtle status shifts

Status shifts can be also indicated by the smallest gestures.

It could be as simple as someone being in charge of the TV remote control.

Or eating the last slice of cake, when both characters are hungry.

Or revealing new information that the others don't know.

Standing up when someone comes into the room, or staying seated when others are standing, is another status display.

Any time a character demonstrates a tiny degree of power, deference, knowledge or mastery, they're subtly changing the status relationships.

The dynamics between characters are full of such shifting energies and impulses.

They can also be seen at close-up level, in the moment-by-moment dialogue between characters.

Look at any page of dialogue, and you'll see subtle status indicators at work.

For example, a character using a lot of tag questions - isn't it? aren't they? - is seeking approval from another. This suggests a degree of deference or uncertainty. Someone with high authority typically uses fewer tag questions.

Women also use tag questions more than men.

Some people ask more questions, while others make more statements.

Some people use a lot of first-person "I" when they speak, whereas others acknowledge other people more, using "you" and "we".

These kinds of speech interaction are the stuff of sociolinguistics - the study of interpersonal language. It reveals fascinating insights about how we negotiate the minefield of social roles, identities and status.

129

It's a great topic for writers. It sheds light on the assumptions underlying every single speech act our characters make.

I was interested to hear that in Japan, speaking to strangers can be challenging, because Japanese speakers use different grammatical forms, depending on the status of the person they're talking to.

It's a social minefield, because status is determined by your job and salary. So if you don't know someone's job status, you don't know how to address them.

But dialogue aside, our individual language is loaded with information about your worldview, your relation to others, your place in society and social group.

Whether you say *Hi! Hello! Good afternoon* or *Yo!* speaks volumes about you (or your characters), and places you socially. Status is everywhere.

Use it to create clear distinctions and tensions between your characters, and then reverse it to shake things up.

TRY THIS:

Looking at your characters in a scene, identify where they get their status from, and the value at stake.

Now, plot the characters in a hierarchy. Who's at the top of the pecking order? Who's down below? Who's ascending, and who's threatened by this?

What's the status quo at the start of your scene, and what's the opposite?

Now, work out how you can create this reversal. What might provoke one character into overturning the pecking order?

Think of secrets to be revealed, new information, different character strengths coming into play.

Plot the beats in your scene needed to effect this change, then write the scene.

TRY THIS:
Analyse the dialogue in a scene from a published script.

Mark up any status indicators, including register, questions, use of names and pronouns, and lines interrupted by others.

Notice who's driving the direction of the dialogue, and any switches in the "baton of power".

Some shifts may be overt assertions of power. For example: "Don't do that!"

Others might be more subtle. For example: "Are you sure that's a good idea?"

Note the different levels of intensity.

Who's in charge of the conversation? Where does this change?

Dialogue is a bit like possession in a ball game. The ball passes back and forth between players, with different moves, kicks and throws. But someone always has the ball.

TRY THIS:
Listen out for status play in conversations around you, at work, with friends, or in the street.

Gather examples of status-rich exchanges to use in your dialogue.

Often, you don't need to use the exact words. Simply identify the impulse and restate it in words of your own.

See also: Secrets, Wants and Stakes.

Further reading:
Johnstone, K. (1979) *Impro: Improvisation and the Theatre*. London, Bloomsbury.

Show and Tell

Fiction writers are usually familiar with the difference between "show" and "tell". You may even be fed up hearing about it!

But it's really worth digging into deeper. "Show" and "tell" are often presented as clear-cut alternatives. In reality, the boundaries are far more blurred.

It's also worth investigating how this works in drama, as the distinction is crucial in what is, after all, "show business". This can provide useful insights.

The show/tell distinction goes back to the ancient Greeks. It's derived from their concepts of mimesis (think of "mimic"), which means "mimicry, enactment" and diegesis ("narration, storytelling"). So, the show/tell distinction was right there in the earliest roots of drama.

As a reminder of "show" and "tell", here's the famous example credited to the Russian author, Anton Chekhov. Note: he wrote both plays and fiction. He wrote:

> *Don't tell me the moon is shining. Show me the*
> *glint of light on broken glass.*

Read it again, slowly. Notice the kind of pictures evoked in your mind by each sentence.

> *Don't tell me the moon is shining. Show me the*
> *glint of light on broken glass.*

In the first sentence, the moon is a big, bold moon high in the sky.

In the second, I'm getting a more elusive, suggestive picture, and a different mood of slight melancholy. Is there a broken window, or a smashed wine glass?

IN SUMMARY:

To "tell" is to give information. It's factual, more detached.

To "show" is to evoke or enact, to bring something to life.

So, when might you use each?

"Telling" is great for cutting to the chase, and sketching in context and setting. If you want to take your audience somewhere fast, a simple "telling" signpost can save a lot of time. The classic fairytale opener, "once upon a time", is a great example of this.

"Telling" can create a sense of detachment. The audience is more aware they're being told a story, so they may be in a more objective or playful relationship to it.

With "showing", on the other hand, a story is experienced more directly, closer. The audience are immersed in it more. They may be situated inside the protagonist's viewpoint, and drawn deep into the character's world, in an almost seductive way. John Gardner describes this almost hypnotic state as the "fictive dream".

This show/tell distinction is probably familiar to you, if you're a fiction writer. And to be clear, there isn't a "good" and "bad" here. There are just different ways to tell stories. Writers make different choices at different times.

However, in dramatic writing, the distinction between "show" and "tell" is significant. It cuts to the heart of what drama is.

"Showing" is essentially the art of dramatization itself.

The root of the word drama is doing, action. Enacting.

"Telling" does still get used in plays and movies. Voiceover, for example, is a kind of telling. But telling is undramatic. Scriptwriters usually look for ways to dramatize wherever possible.

So, let's look at show and tell through the lens of drama.

133

Show/tell in drama

In his *Poetics*, Aristotle makes a distinction between tragedy and poetry which is linked to show and tell. In his day, tragedy used the immersive technique of "showing". It brought the audience close to the action. Poetry used epic storytelling techniques, a bit like long folk ballads do. He saw poetry as an inferior art form.

Aristotle saw tragedy as economical and powerful, bringing audiences right into the middle of the action to witness events directly. This helped them to move them more easily to catharsis, which was the point of tragedy.

Epic poetry, meanwhile, told sweeping stories which jumped around in time and place, holding the audience at a distance. They weren't moved to experience emotional catharsis to the same degree.

Aristotle's *Poetics* might well be the source of the notion that showing is somehow "better" than telling.

But the truth is, they're simply different techniques, with different pros and cons. Each has been in favour at different times, and for different reasons.

For example, in the 1700s, in France, playwrights admired the classical Greek ideals. So they favoured the dramatic unities, and mimesis or "showing".

But English playwrights of the time, including Shakespeare, used all sorts of epic storytelling devices, including frame narrators, songs, dances, and plays-within-plays. In modern terminology, they were happy to breach the invisible "fourth wall" between the audience and the play.

The late 1800s saw the start of the Naturalism movement. Epic, anti-realism techniques once again fell out of favour. The aim was to represent gritty real life. In drama, audiences were encouraged to forget they were in a theatre.

But telling came back into fashion in the modern era, notably in the Epic theatre of the German playwright, Bertolt Brecht.

Brecht wrote plays full of songs, asides, storytelling and other techniques. He wanted to prevent the audience from getting too emotionally involved. He sought to achieve an estrangement or alienation effect (Verfremdungseffekt), to keep them at a critically detached distance.

In Brecht's view, the emotional style of naturalistic theatre was shallow and manipulative. He was writing at a time between the two world wars. He wanted to alert people to the dangers of being swept away emotionally by powerful storytelling, and aimed to draw attention to the story mechanisms at work.

So, while Aristotle looked down on epic storytelling techniques, Brecht saw them as highly desirable.

This is a useful reminder that not all writers aim for "suspension of disbelief" and hypnotizing readers. You need to choose your narrative form mindfully, for good reasons.

And in any case, it's too simplistic to consider "show" and "tell" as opposites. The different storytelling techniques can happily be combined, mixed and matched.

For example, take verbatim drama. In verbatim, writers create a script from people's authentic speech, so there's an aspiration towards realism. But verbatim plays often use a highly theatrical production style, with epic techniques such as song. An example is the UK National Theatre production, *London Road*, which has also been produced as a film. It's an unusual hybrid of documentary material and musical storytelling about a real-life murderer. It uses a combination of epic techniques along with direct verbatim testimony from the London Road community.

See also: Time, Fourth Wall, Physicality, Verbatim.

Spectacle

Spectacle is one of the seven pillars of dramatic technique described in Aristotle's *Poetics*. In Greek, it's called *opsis* (what is seen).

Aristotle regarded spectacle as the least important of the dramatic elements, even a bit lowly. He called it "the least artistic". It's possible he was slightly snobbish about craftspeople able to impress the masses with fancy scenery. He preferred the writerly poetic arts of *mythos* (plot) and *lexis* (diction).

However, spectacle is one of the most powerful tools at any writer's disposal, so it can't be written off that easily.

And within the visual media of film and stage, its impact counts even more.

I've met several set designers during productions, and the way they think and create is incredibly inspiring. Their art is far more than creating a spectacular visual impact. They dive deep into the themes of the script, the characters, the world of the story, history, visual art, material and textures. They create a visual world that heightens the story and excites the audience's senses.

When you know how much effort and thought goes into creating a set design, it's a small step to realizing the potential for thinking about your own writing.

However, it's important first of all to understand the distinction between spectacle and dramatic action.

Spectacle without an underlying dramatic motive or driving emotion is likely to feel empty. That may be partly what Aristotle was getting at.

But properly aligned to dramatic action and theme, spectacle is incredibly powerful.

Firstly, don't underestimate the power of the outsize, the heightened, the exotic, the unfamiliar and the familiar.

Anything extreme, unusual, novel or relevant to the audience will attract attention. These are the same values that journalists use to choose news stories. They include superlatives – for example: *first, last, best, biggest, brightest, fastest*. And they include anything with a direct impact on the audience, anything that chimes with them.

So, anything that excites the imagination or ticks the "recognition" box will attract attention.

When it comes to spectacle, we're especially drawn to see familiar environments disrupted by novel behaviour, such as James Bond speedboat chasing along the River Thames. Or novel locations, such as aliens in South Africa, in the movie *District 9*. We're also drawn to novel scenarios, such as the alien first contact through the lens of linguistics in *Arrival*. And to transgressive use of iconic locations, such as James Bond charging through the Grand Bazaar in Istanbul.

TRY THIS:

Taking an ordinary scene from your work in progress, develop the setting and how your characters interact with it.

Is there an element of transgression, of disruption of rules and norms?

Is the setting visually exciting, and familiar to some of the audience?

What status quo does the setting represent, and can this be disrupted?

Looking at your setting with eyes half shut, what stands out as iconic or emblematic? Can this be distilled and amplified?

I was at a production of *An Inspector Calls* in London where the audience applauded the ingenious set.

The house interior was mounted on stalks within the vast stage, creating a world-within-a-world feel. It collapsed spectacularly at a key dramatic moment, and was highly memorable.

If the audience clapped at your spectacular visual idea, how would you feel?

How important is spectacle for you, among the elements of dramatic technique?

How might you harness this thinking to your work in progress?

See also: Physicality, Objects, Transformation.

Improv

Improvisation - also called "improv" or "impro" - is a spontaneous form of performance. It has a long history. In the 17th-18th century, for example, Italians enjoyed *commedia dell'arte*, where actors improvised on a familiar story, using set-piece comic turns.

Contemporary improv came to the fore through the work of theatre director Keith Johnstone. His book Impro is a treasure chest of ideas that are just as useful for writers as for actors.

One of the most useful improv concepts for writers is the idea of saying "yes" to ideas that come along.

Often, we're trained to defend ourselves against incoming ideas and say "no," or have a critical response that shuts things down.

In improv, performers have to be open to incoming suggestions, known as "offers", and accept and work with them.

This means that if your co-performer suddenly offers the suggestion that a huge elephant is sitting on your toes, you agree. You incorporate this new fact into your shared reality, and develop it further.

For most people, this kind of acceptance is difficult, and actors need considerable training to get comfortable with it.

As writers, we're used to preferring our own agendas, and not wanting to follow those of others. Improv calls for unusual generosity towards your fellow creatives. Actors can't just come up with a good idea and then bend the scene to their will. They need to be truly collaborative.

The idea of acceptance and openness to others' ideas can really benefit your writing. It may seem to be the opposite of the conflict we're used to from other dramatic paradigms. However, it offers different scope for tension and momentum.

Where does this tension come from?

Firstly, improvised dialogue is unpredictable. Improv performance gets tension from surprise, freshness and randomness.

When two performers meet, they have no way of knowing what the other will say. No one side controls the conversation. So, their interaction lives in a fluid space where the subconscious and surprises are allowed to flourish.

Tension comes from the genuine anticipation of surprise by not just the audience, but also the performers. This is an extraordinarily daring and demanding kind of creativity, with its inherent paradox of "create, now!", and the need to resist resistance.

If ever there was a practice capable of exploding the notion of creative block, it's improv.

Puppets, masks, the subconscious

Writers may struggle with impro, as we're used to asserting a viewpoint and shaping stories to suit our egos and agendas. But it's well worth exploring what impro can bring to the table.

Often, when we write, we try to edit at the same time, effectively clamping a lid on deviation, and often on inspiration, too.

Impro asks us to set aside the judging, cognitive part of our brains, and accept our primal impulses.

If you need a great example of the spontaneous and the controlled in creative conflict, look online for videos by the ventriloquist Nina Conti. Her work shows the two impulses side by side, interacting with each other in hilarious and often unsettling fashion.

The split personalities of Nina's puppet characters and MC persona switch back and forth with astonishing speed. Her puppet characters (including guest humans wearing masks) seem to show the taboo, subconscious mind, while Nina "herself" leads them in conversation. The different identities all come from the same performer, raising fascinating questions about the subconscious mind and how it's usually suppressed. The puppet characters provide a conduit for often unspoken and taboo topics.

TRY THIS:

Sit at your writing desk, and use your usual writing hand for one voice. Shift to a slightly different position to represent a different voice.

Write a dialogue between the two voices, allowing the two distinct sides to speak and come through.

Try not to censor or judge. See what emerges.

Are the two personalities combative? Are they distinct? Does anything surprise you? Does it feel different, writing in this way?

Explore using this feeling to write more freely.

Verbatim

Verbatim is a technique for interviewing others and gathering their language to put into scripts.

Verbatim has some common ground with improv, in that you need to be open to what emerges, rather than bend it to your writer's iron will.

So, they both call for an openness to experience, and the joy and surprise of unfiltered communication. So if you're a writer with limited range, verbatim techniques can help to open your eyes and ears – to new characters, voices and rhythms of language.

In verbatim drama, the writer will typically interview others, harvest their language, and compile and edit it into a script for performance. An example is the verbatim musical and movie starring Olivia Coleman, *London Road*.

Even if you don't want to go full-on verbatim, you can definitely benefit from interviewing contributors on your chosen theme, and learn how they tick.

People will always surprise you. You may have the clearest story in the world, a strong idea of your characters and their wants, and a pile of research into the social/ cultural/ historical background.

You know what you want to say. However, this can be dangerous. Your crystal-clear agenda can make for predictable, preachy writing.

It can make all the difference to interview others who have a different, authentic viewpoint on your theme, and a distinctive voice that's not yours.

It'll allow you to get beyond the confines of your own preconceptions and language, and be surprised and illuminated by what others have to say.

Of course, you've probably talked to others who are interested in your topic. But that's not the same as deep listening and gathering, and openness to viewpoints and language that aren't your own.

Verbatim technique is a bit like being a documentary film maker, and being open to situations that unfold as you encounter them. When you ask questions and respond, don't judge the contributions you're offered. They may not chime with your viewpoint, but they'll help you form a rich and multi-dimensional view of a complex theme.

TRY THIS:
Record an interview with someone who's steeped in the topic of your script.

Rather than trying to imagine what they think, listen to what they say: their language, register, turns of phrase, self-interruptions, idiosyncrasies.

Write these down, with all their fragments, interruptions and anomalies. Often, it's exactly these qualities that help characters spring to life.

Looking at your notes, does anything jump out at you? Trouble you? Make you think?

It's likely these elements are a clue to distinctive characters and voices. Explore where you can make use of them in your scripts.

Sometimes, a single telling line of truth has more impact than many lines of invented dialogue. Does anything you've gathered astonish you, or seem salient in this way?

TRY THIS:
Keep a notebook of phrases and interactions from people you encounter around you.

Pick something that really jumps out to you, and analyze why it has this effect. What are its qualities of imagery, observation, truth, economy, rhythm?

If you substitute single words, is the phrase or exchange still as effective?

Staying alert to random interactions and phrases for your notebook will keep your creative well full and ideas percolating in your subconscious.

See also: Johnstone, Mental Spaces.

Further reading:
Hammond, W. and Steward, D. (eds) (2008) *Verbatim Verbatim: Contemporary Documentary Theatre*. London, Oberon Books.

Secrets

Secrets play a major role in dramatic technique.

Playwright Arthur Miller said that "every play is the story of birds coming home to roost". He was putting secrets right at the heart of all drama.

Secrets are so crucial in drama that they even have their own technical name: dramatic irony, which is covered elsewhere in this book.

So, what's the great power of secrets?

Firstly, everyone has secrets they'd rather not share. So, everyone can relate to the idea of having a public self and a private self.

Some secrets stay buried, and others become revealed. When and where secrets are revealed can have a great impact on characters.

Imagine finding out something powerful about someone close to you. Something they've been carrying around with them alone for years.

A powerful revelation can entirely change how you see that person. It might help to explain why they behave as they do.

You might view them with greater empathy. Or, you might suddenly see them as a horrible creature.

Whichever way round, the person's identity has been shattered for you, and this can be traumatic. Sometimes, we may have to recalibrate our whole understanding of that person and our relationship.

If the person is close to us, such as a family member, a huge revelation can even undermine our own sense of identity.

Secrets can be heavy, like massive boulders. When they're passed on, it's a relief for the carrier. But then, someone else has to bear or share the burden.

Secrets can never be untold. Once out of the box, they're out to stay. They also have a way of spreading, of dissipating.

If you confide in someone, it's no longer a secret. And they won't take the secrecy nearly as seriously as you do. It'll be far more easily passed on, until before you know it, the whole neighbourhood knows.

Secrets are physical

Secrets aren't simply factual information.

Secrets turn us into bubbling, fermenting pots with ill-fitting lids. Sometimes the lids rattle and steam escapes. It might be a full-on emotional outburst. Or, it might be what's known in poker as a "tell", when an undercurrent of truth slips to the surface.

Traumatic buried secrets can have a lasting effect on a person's body. If trauma can't be released safely, through the natural fight-or-flight mechanism, then it can stay embodied for many years.

The effects of trauma can also be clearly seen in animals who have been abused or experienced shock. They're much less able to understand and integrate it than humans.

The physical strain of keeping shameful secrets can also be tremendous. Some people develop tics or avoidance behaviours through the stress of unresolved trauma.

Other secrets are more joyous - a secret love, for example.

The word "secret" derives from a Latin word for "separate, set apart". This highlights the divisive nature of secrets. People stand on opposite sides of a wall: knowing, and not knowing.

145

This echoes the relationship between audience and performers. Sometimes, there is collusion and sharing. At other times, there's a fourth wall between them. So, secrets are the perfect mechanism for stage drama, where there's tension between illusion and reality, between pretence, truth, and all the stages in between.

With every secret, a good question to ask is: "why not be open?"

Who is the character keeping the secret from, and why?

Do the other characters wish to be told, or would they prefer not to know?

What do they feel when they find out? Shocked, horrified, relieved, thrilled? Do they now go on to share the burden? Or do they pass on the secret?

For some people, secrets are a way of maintaining control, especially for people who have low status. A child, for example, might compensate for a lack of privacy and personal space by keeping secrets, or by developing a secret world that belongs only to them.

In this sense, a secret can be extraordinarily precious.

Secrets are connected to gossip. Sometimes, people enjoy finding out secrets and passing them on. This is thought to be an important part of human bonding. Anyone who is too secretive and doesn't reveal much will intrigue others, but struggle to get close to them.

What's the difference between secrets and dramatic irony?

Dramatic irony is a specific kind of secret - one that has been set up by the dramatist, for the audience to enjoy.

TRY THIS:

Thinking about your main character, imagine they have a powerful secret. What is it? Is the secret about them, or someone else?

What behaviour or actions make you aware that they have a secret? What gives them away?

What would they hate for others to know about them? What would happen if others knew? How would they deal with vulnerability?

If the secret is about someone else, how well do they keep it? Do they have a moral code around secrecy? Do they enjoy being someone's confidant, or not?

In what circumstances, or under what pressure, might they give away someone's secret?

Would they feel guilty, or shake off any guilt with ease?

TRY THIS:
Brainstorm secrets you know. Are they about you, or about someone else?

Imagine a busy event - a big conference, a family gathering - where a secret is announced. What does it feel like to have the secret broadcast in public?

If it's about you, would you brazen it out, or be mortified and shrink away?

How do age, maturity and experience affect your relationship to secrets?

Would you lie to keep a secret? Or just maintain silence?

What's the biggest secret you've ever kept?

What's the biggest secret you've ever blurted out?

Explore the dramatic potential of secrets and reveals.

See also: Dramatic Irony.

147

Dramatic Irony

If a scene has dramatic irony, it means the audience knows more than the characters.

Technically, it creates a kind of suspense. And that's powerfully engaging. So it's a useful tool in your writing toolkit.

For example, the audience has seen the evil antagonist plant a bomb under the table. Most characters don't know about it, but the audience does. So there's a delicious tension. We're curious about what will happen when they find out.

From a writing viewpoint, dramatic irony means priming the audience with knowledge.

For example, you show the baddie planting the bomb under the table.

The scene is then primed with built-in tension. The audience are on the edge of their seats, wondering what's going to happen when someone finds the bomb. This gives a rising arc shape to the whole scene.

For example: a husband finds an incriminating love letter to his wife, and hides it in his pocket. He decides that, rather than confronting her, he'll bide his time.

When he next speaks to her, the whole conversation is primed with his hidden knowledge.

We're squealing inside with the agony of what might happen.

The whole scene gains delicious tension from our foreknowledge.

With dramatic irony, the audience is in on a secret. They're one step ahead of the characters, and get to enjoy that superior knowledge, sense of collusion, and suspense.

Kinds of dramatic irony

There are different kinds of dramatic irony.

Sometimes, every character is in on the secret, apart from one. For example, the poor husband in the above example, whose wife has a lover.

The whole neighbourhood has known about his wife's lover for years. The husband is the only one still in the dark. In this instance, the audience is in the same position as the wife, lover and entire neighbourhood.

In the other example, with the bomb planted under the table, only the baddie knows about it. And he's long fled from the scene. Everyone else is in the dark. In this instance, the audience has the same knowledge as the villain, and feels a growing sense of horror and helplessness at being unable to warn the others.

Often, characters in the same scene have different degrees of knowledge, which creates different dynamics.

For example, take the woman with the secret lover – let's call her "Liz" – and the oblivious husband, Bill. Say Liz's best friend, Marcie, finds out about the lover. She can't tell Bill. Her next coffee catchup with Liz will be fraught with tension.

In Marcie's eyes, Liz's display of marital happiness will seem horribly hollow. Bill's will seem pathetic and poignant. Along with Marcie, we'll be torn between emotions of anger, sympathy, frustration; wanting to intervene but being unable to; and, as members of the audience, dying to know how it plays out.

Dramatic irony creates powerful tension, by opening a knowledge gap between characters and audience. It makes us wait on tenterhooks for the exciting moment when the character finds out the truth. We enjoy their reaction all the more, because of this anticipation.

There are examples of dramatic irony everywhere, going right back to Greek tragedy.

Think of Oedipus, blissfully unaware that he was marrying his mother.

In his case, the secret overhangs the entire story, and the audience knows the truth long before Oedipus has even an inkling. It's an incredibly powerful structure. In fact, Oedipus is often described as "the most ironic play ever performed".

At other times, the writer sets up a secret just for a particular scene.

Take Act V scene 1 of Shakespeare's *Hamlet* - the one with the skull.

Just before the scene happens, we learn that Hamlet's girlfriend, Ophelia, has drowned. We know she has died. Hamlet doesn't. This foreknowledge primes the scene.

We see Hamlet arriving back in the country, unaware of this terrible news. He comes across a gravedigger at work. We, the audience, know it's Ophelia's grave. Hamlet doesn't.

The whole scene is overcast with awful anticipation of the moment when Hamlet finds out.

In this scene, Shakespeare really twists the knot. Hamlet repeatedly asks: "Whose grave is this?", and never gets a straight answer. The gravedigger clowns around, digging up a skull that grimly foreshadows the news to come.

When Hamlet eventually finds out about Ophelia's death (by which time we're squirming in our seats), Shakespeare doesn't simply have a character blurt out the news. There's no sudden rush of exposition, as in: "Yes, sorry to break the news. It's Ophelia's grave".

Instead, he twists the knot still more, with the arrival of distant bells - a funeral cortege arriving. As it draws closer, we see the grieving royal family. And slowly, for poor tortured Hamlet, the penny drops.

It's a wonderfully moving scene, full of tension and torment, and achieves extraordinary power through its use of dramatic irony.

TRY THIS:
Any moment when a character finds out key information is a turning point. You can exploit this by handling these moments carefully and sparingly.

Revelations of secrets are like small grenades for the characters. Each one changes the status quo, shifts the balance of power.

So, rather than letting every grenade explode at once, manage their impact by keeping something back. This is known as "withholding".

You can stage withholding to allow different characters to find things out at different times. Maybe one character is allowed to know, but not the others? Then a second character finds out, so that two are in collusion, but the others are still in the dark?

You can also show knowledge being concealed and revealed in different ways.

For example, you could use a physical or visual approach, such as an incriminating visual, letter or evidence. In Tom Stoppard's *The Real Thing* (1982), a handkerchief provides evidence of an affair, echoing a similar technique used in Othello.

Or, you could include the revelation in the dialogue, with one character revealing a secret to another.

As well as exploring how characters might reveal secrets, it's also good to explore why.

What's the reason for telling the secret - the dramatic action? Those reasons might be benign, but they could also be the opposite. When someone reveals a secret, is it an act of bonding, protection, pity, release, revenge, collusion?

See also: Secrets, Status.

Obligatory Scene

An "obligatory scene" is a concept from screenwriting. The expression comes from the French scène à faire (a scene which must be made), referring to a scene which is so expected by the audience that the writer is obliged to provide it.

Typically, it's the climactic moment when the protagonist and antagonist have their final encounter.

Classic examples of obligatory scenes can be seen in Western films such as *High Noon*, where the two main characters go head-to-head in a final dramatic stand-off.

In this familiar trope, you might see the "black hat" and the "white hat" close in on each other, hands hovering over holsters, audience tension at an agonising high as we wait to see who will win the gunfight.

If you deny the audience this "obligatory" scene, they may well be disappointed.

In story terms, this kind of scene is far more than a shoot-out between two enemies. It's a decisive symbolic moment in the film structure.

It's the moment when the two opposing forces embodied by the characters fight to prevail.

The stakes aren't just the survival of the characters, but also the moral values of the story.

Of course, obligatory scenes are by no means obligatory, and we'll consider other approaches later in this section.

But for now, let's focus on the conventional obligatory scene.

Time-stretching

The obligatory climactic scene often ends with a death. But not an ordinary death - a slow, drawn-out, agonising one.

It's very rare to see the protagonist dispatch their enemy with a quick, effective shot to the temple, or have the enemy keel over and bite the dust in an instant.

A final death scene often stretches far beyond the bounds of realism.

But this isn't just to give the lead actors a meaty, emotional exchange to get their teeth into. It's to give this scene the full dramatic impact it needs to complete the story arc.

If the end of the story arc isn't given due importance, it won't stand out as memorable and meaningful. If it's over in a trice, you deny the audience the chance to process what it means. It's like saying "the end, over and out", without the satisfaction of enjoying the moment.

So, the writer often needs to stretch time, to give due prominence to the final confrontation.

Theme

With a climactic obligatory scene, it's not just the story arc that's at stake. It's the whole theme and morality of the world.

The end of the arc marks the end of the protagonist's transformational journey. Structurally, it's like a load-bearing tent pole that carries the essence of the whole edifice.

Taken together, the beginning and end of a story encapsulate its theme. You can grasp the theme in a simplified way, just by looking at those moments.

If the protagonist starts out a victim and ends up triumphant, it's a story about battling to overcome, a story about heroism.

If the protagonist starts out as top dog and ends up in the gutter, it's a story about hubris or the dangers of ambition or power.

If the protagonist starts out as reviled and ends up loved, it's a story about acceptance or redemption.

While this is admittedly over-simplistic, deciding the story bookends can provide a really helpful thumbnail of your story shape and theme.

This can act as a compass, and help to prevent the side-tracking and blind alleys that can happen when you're deep in the detail of the writing.

This simplified shape also reveals a lot about how you see the world. It's like a lens into your world view.

If you're an optimist, you're more likely to have an upward trajectory between the two story poles. If you're a pessimist, it's more likely the poles will be reversed.

A circular structure where the character transforms, then ends up back where they started from, might suggest a belief in the power of fate.

Take a look at the beginning and end of your main character's journey, and see what it reveals.

From a writer's viewpoint, it can be challenging to come up with an obligatory scene that's fresh and interesting. So many have been written before that it's hard to find something new to present.

Indeed, some writers find the concept of an obligatory scene so clichéd that they go out of their way to avoid one.

In the Coen brothers' film, *No Country for Old Men*, about a sheriff hunting down a killer, the escalating tension leads us to expect a massive showdown between the two. However, this never happens. The villain gets away.

This denial of expectation is so unusual that the film's ending is seen as controversial, and is much discussed. The lack of easy closure seems to suggest a world where justice can't be relied on, where there are no comforting certainties.

The "hero's journey" type of story, with a clear moral trajectory, is more common in older and conventional films.

In some ways, they reflect a time when life and morality, good and evil, were seen in a simpler way.

In more recent films, moral codes are often less clear, and characters more ambiguous and complex. As faith in justice, leaders and establishment institutions has crumbled, the prevalent story shapes have also changed.

So, although obligatory scenes are usual, and audiences tend to be disappointed if they don't get one, be aware that they aren't the only option.

Be aware, however, that an audience's experience of a story is disproportionately affected by the ending.

If you set up strong emotional expectations which have nowhere to go, the audience may not experience catharsis or release. They may find the story frustrating and unresolved - not just intellectually and emotionally, but also physically.

A climactic obligatory scene usually takes place close to the end of a story, as the emotional high point between the opposing forces.

But the story rarely stops dead after the obligatory scene. An abrupt ending at this point would feel wrong. A story needs a sense of closure - a kind of epilogue, to tie up the ends.

This is catharsis in action. The reader has experienced an emotional high point, and needs some time to process and come down from it.

Only then are they released from their emotional journey.

So, in a way, the epilogue moment at the end of a story is a kind of obligatory scene.

See also: Catharsis, Fatal Flaw.

Catharsis

The word catharsis comes from early Greek drama, and was used by Aristotle in his influential *Poetics*.

In its original sense, catharsis meant a kind of purging - a physical cleansing.

Aristotle used the "purging" metaphor to describe the emotional experience audiences underwent when they watched a tragic play. A tragedy was seen as a kind of safety valve for strong emotions, such as pity and fear.

In modern psychological terms, it's like putting your reader through trauma, but by proxy, at a safe remove from real experience. The trauma can be remotely experienced and released through tears, laughter and discharged tension.

So, psychologically, hearing a story is a kind of ritual, involving the manipulation of tension, and leading – at least in Aristotle's time – to catharsis.

Usually, the moment of catharsis is near the end of a long journey - the emotional climax of your story. It's when the tension built over the course of the story is finally released.

It's when Cinderella falls into the arms of her prince.

It's when Scrooge wakes up to Christmas morning, a changed man.

It's when the school pupils stand up on their desks in *Dead Poets Society* to support their teacher.

It's when the transformational journey of the characters is completed.

This moment is the reason for the story. To put it another way, it's the story's promise to the audience. It's so important it might well be an "obligatory scene".

So as a writer, you'll want to check that your story has a climactic moment of catharsis for the audience.

If you're a "pantser", flying by the seat of your pants, get to the end of your story. Then look back and check for a sense of catharsis, and whether the journey builds effectively to get there.

If you're a plotter, you could even plan your story backwards, from the end. This isn't as strange as it sounds. Many screenwriters and novelists do this.

When you're next watching a film and experience catharsis, take time to notice those feelings, and analyse what caused them. Note specifics, and see if there's anything you can use for your current work in progress.

Mostly, catharsis is experienced at the end of a story.

But sometimes, you might find yourself reacting in a similarly powerful way to events in the middle of a story.

Everyone experiences stories differently, but maybe you've watched a film or play (or listened to music) that suddenly got under your radar in an inexplicable way, and made you cry?

Somehow, the story has tapped into something buried, and helped to release it.

As a writer, it's good to watch out for these emotions, and interrogate them. It may be a sign of something you don't fully understand. It can give clues to themes that resonate strongly with you. Take a close look at this kind of moment, and see if you can identify what its ingredients are.

If I find myself crying while writing (which can be messy!), it's a good sign. I know I've tapped into something that might hit others, too.

That said, not everyone believes that catharsis is a necessary part of the writer's job. Some writers reject the idea, and write stories that deliberately aren't resolved, leaving the audience without release, as in *No Country for Old Men*.

This might be because the writers want to challenge or subvert traditional story structure. Or they want the audience to feel unease, even distress, at the lack of emotional closure in the ending. Which can also be a clever way to make the film echo in their audience's minds, long after they've left the cinema.

If you're interested in knowing more about this area, look up the "Zeigarnik Effect" and the psychology of closure online.

And catharsis or not, pay great attention to your ending and its emotional impact, as this will be the lasting impression your readers take away.

See also: Tension, Transformation, Iglesias, Marks, Obligatory Scene.

Fourth Wall

In drama, the "fourth wall" is an imaginary, invisible wall between the audience and the actors.

In performances in the tradition of realism – most movies, and many stage plays – actors pretend they can't see the audience. They perform with each other, within the self-contained world of the play. They don't directly acknowledge the audience's existence.

But when they break the "fourth wall", the performers reach out and speak directly to the audience, disrupting the imaginary membrane between them.

You can see this in TV shows including *Fleabag* and *Malcolm in the Middle*, where the main character turns and speaks to the viewer. But the technique is not just used for comedy. It can also be highly chilling. For example, Frances Underwood in *House of Cards* speaks out directly to viewers in sinister asides. In Shakespeare's *Othello*, the evil Iago speaks out to the audience about his plans.

A character "aside" to the audience – just a quick quip – or even a knowing wink are also fourth wall breaches.

A fourth wall breach instantly creates a very different kind of audience relationship.

It reminds the audience that they're watching a story. And they know it. The performance is an illusion. A fourth wall breach puts the audience more at a distance. They're less immersed, and less likely to be swept away. They're more detached emotionally.

What's more, a fourth wall breach puts the audience on a more equal footing with the performers. They're in on the secret. There's a greater sense of parity, of collusion, between the audience and the performers. They're acknowledged as intellectual equals.

The German dramatist Bertolt Brecht was well known for his use of fourth wall breaches and other "alienation effects", including music and song.

Shakespeare also broke the fourth wall frequently. At the end of *A Midsummer Night's Dream*, Puck sends the audience home with a direct-address epilogue. The evil Iago in Othello and the king in Henry V also address the audience. Sometimes the effect of direct address is chilling, sometimes it's comedic.

So, how might you use this technique?

Firstly, be aware that direct address creates a distinct relationship with your audience. It's a powerful convention, and needs to be used with great care.

Once you've established the direct address convention, you need to follow it through and ideally develop, twist or escalate it, so that it has its own story point.

With direct address, you're no longer hypnotizing the audience deep into your world, presenting it as real.

Instead, you're saying "this is a story". The character speaking to the audience becomes their guide and colluder. They're implicitly the "partner in crime" of evil Iago or Underwood, or the frustrated teenage Malcolm.

This direct hotline to the characters can be hugely engaging for audiences. However, it can come at a price:

- Pausing the story for direct address can slow the pace (or increase the tension, depending on your view).
- Self-consciousness can become irritating if it's overused (or refreshingly playful).
- If we're aware it's just a story, we might not care as much about the characters. We might not be as invested.

160

With fourth wall breaches, you should also be aware of the power relationship at work between you and the audience.

Do you want to hypnotize or seduce them, plant vivid pictures in their heads? Get them laughing and crying along with your characters?

Or do you want to draw attention to the illusion of storytelling, and engage with them in a playful, collusive way? Do you want to unsettle them with an unreliable narrator who casts a doubt on the whole edifice of story, and the power of storytellers?

How do you see your readers? As equals, as knowing fellow travellers? Or as your attentive audience, to be swayed and manipulated.

Though of course, they can also be manipulated by a knowing narrator!

Your chosen viewpoint is a powerful expression of status, and this can be seen more clearly when it's out there, dramatized.

Finally, in a fun meta-twist, fourth walls also appear in stories of their own.

Shakespeare said that "all the world's a stage, and all the men and women merely players". His suggestion was that we're all putting on a performance, all the time. This metaphor was developed by the sociologist Ervin Goffman, and is discussed in a later chapter.

But much earlier, the Greek philosopher Plato ploughed right through the fourth wall in his *Allegory of the Cave*. In this story, he imagines the human condition as being like prisoners chained in a cave, seeing only shadows cast by a fire on the walls. He thought human perceptions were limited, and we are unable to see the true nature of reality. Plato's theme is also explored in the film *The Matrix*.

On a comedy note, Woody Allen plays with multiple fourth walls and meta narrative in many of his films. The plays of Tim Crouch, including *An Oak Tree* and *I, Malvolio*, play in a knowing way with narrative frames.

Fourth walls are all around, ready to be breached! How might you plough through the fourth wall in your writing?

161

TRY THIS:

If you're writing fiction, try inviting your reader into your world more overtly. Use storytelling techniques to set up a frame narrative at the start.

How does this make you feel as a writer? Note your thoughts about manipulation, (mis)direction, your role and status as a storyteller.

What effect does this have on the reader's relationship with your story?

What are you giving away in the story by revealing its artifice? What are you enriching?

TRY THIS:

Brainstorm ideas for pushing the fourth wall idea to an extreme.

What's lost and gained if your characters breach the fourth wall? What happens if you reveal secrets and confide in the audience?

Explore what you lose and gain if the audience can see your transparent mechanisms at work.

See also: Show and Tell, Status, Goffman.

Transformation

Transformation is a powerful concept in dramatic technique. Drama's emphasis on the visual means that scriptwriters are used to thinking boldly about transformation, often building it into the fabric of their structure from the start. Transformation can be used as a structuring device at the level of both story and scene.

Transformation goes by different names in different genres. You might hear a fiction editor asking: "How does the character change?" or about the "character arc". In Greek drama, Aristotle refers to *peripeteia* or "reversal" - a sudden change in fortune.

Strategists sometimes talk about a "pivot" - a kind of U-turn.

The essence of transformation is a gradual development, followed by decisive change.

A psychologist might describe this as pattern forming, followed by pattern disruption.

Our brains are wired to look out for patterns which help us to compartmentalize the overwhelming chaos of the world, and make sense of it. These patterns can be visual, aural, tactile, or simply the security of a routine or ritual.

Our brains are on hyper-alert for pattern disruption. When a pattern is formed and then disrupted, we're woken up from our restful complacency. After all, disruption spells danger. It creates adrenaline, which can come from excitement or fear.

163

In the early caveman days, being super-alert to disruption could save our lives. A novel smell or sound could signal a poisonous plant, sabre-tooth tiger or marauding enemy tribesman. So, our bodies have evolved to devote attention towards disruptive experiences.

Nowadays, there aren't any sabre-tooth tigers and the stakes are usually less life-threatening. However, pattern disruption still triggers a touch of adrenaline-fueled fight-or-flight in our primitive lizard brains.

As a writer, you can exploit this natural tendency by disrupting the smooth course of your story. Shake things up for your characters. Don't let them (or your readers) settle into complacency.

TRY THIS:

Look at the setting of one of your scenes. Brainstorm ways that it could change, transform or be disrupted. Think about the possibilities of weather, decor, new ownership, change of use, demolition, rebuilding, tidying, upturning, occupation, emptying, infestation.

Are these changes sudden, or over a long time?

If they're sudden, can they be shown in a single scene?

If they're durational, can before and after be shown in different scenes?

What happens if you put the before and after in a different order?

TRY THIS:

Choose a scene with a significant object or item of clothing. Brainstorm ways the item can be transformed, compiling a list of verbs: distress, dismantle, complete, flatten, expand, shrink.

What are the opposites of these verbs? Which of these transformations can be easily shown and dramatized?

Which transformations are more internal, through character change, and how can you dramatize them? Which come from external events, such as weather or conflict? Which are unnatural or supernatural?

What transformations take place over a long duration or evolution, rather than a sudden disruption? How might this be dramatized?

See also: Objects.

Further reading: Marks, D. (2007) *Inside Story: The Power of the Transformational Arc.* Three Mountains Press.

PART II

Dramatic Thinkers

This section covers an eclectic group of inspiring thinkers and writers who are influential in dramatic thinking.

They aren't necessarily the "usual suspects" (for example, Brecht isn't included, as he's so often discussed elsewhere). But with all these writers, I've had at least one big "aha" moment which has massively helped my writing.

Some of these writers come from the worlds of drama or screenwriting. Others come from psychology, sociology and even philosophy and architecture.

Some are by no means an easy read, but so mind-bending that it's absolutely worth it.

These overviews are my personal takeaways. They'll give you a sense of my key discoveries from reading these writers, so you can decide for yourself whether you want to dig deeper.

Konstantin Stanislavski

KEY TAKEAWAYS

- Stanislavski's theories are behind "method acting", an actor training style famously associated with Marlon Brando and Robert De Niro.
- Stanislavski's work *An Actor Prepares* has been highly influential in dramatic writing as well as acting.
- He encouraged actors to think in terms of interior motivations, and actions, beats and units.
- He encouraged inside-out thinking about character.

Konstantin Stanislavski (1863-1938) was a legendary Russian theatre director famous for his system of actor training, now known as "method acting".

When method acting reached the USA, it became associated with the "authentic" style of actors such as Marlon Brando, Robert De Niro and Dustin Hoffman.

Stanislavski was disaffected with the mannered acting of his time, and interested in a more naturalistic approach. He encouraged actors to make use of memories from their own lives in preparing their roles, to experience the emotions directly, rather than represent them.

170

Stanislavski's major work is *An Actor Prepares*. In this, he describes a process for breaking down scenes into short sections which he called "beats". Although this was simply his Russian pronunciation of "bits", this has become standard terminology in scriptwriting. One common usage is the "beat sheet" - a list of the individual dramatic actions in a scene.

The process of breaking down a scene is sometimes called "uniting". Stanislavski's method helped actors to identify a task or action for each beat, together with its underlying motivation.

Remember the actor's question "what's my motivation?" It comes from Stanislavski's teaching.

In Stanislavski's view, breaking the dialogue into beats helps actors to explore the dramatic and emotional intention of each line, and understand the transitions. This helps the scene to flow with psychological logic when it's put back together.

Beats are an invaluable concept for scriptwriters, as they provide a useful sub-unit for discussing and writing scenes.

They can alert you to any words or moments that are simply hovering in space, rather than motivated by a strong impulse.

Impulses can be physical, such as opens the door, crosses the room. Or they can be an inner impulse, such as reveals the secret, soothes the child.

Movie beat sheets can list bigger chunks of action, such as asks for a pay rise. This might take several minutes of dialogue. Or, units might be smaller units of action: welcomes the visitor, takes off the coat. Beats can also change within lines of dialogue: "Hello, come in! No, hang on – let's go out."

Beats are perhaps best understood as small shifts in energy or intention. They can help you stand back from the word level of a script, and see its emotional journey more clearly.

I use Stanislavski's thinking when I edit my scripts.

For example, if any speeches seem wordy or muddy in their intention, I break them up using slashes / and try to understand the impulse beneath the words.

In a way, it's a bit like annotating a piece of music you want to play, and inserting dynamics. It helps you to clarify the interpretation and emotional journey of the piece, and tell the story more expressively.

See also: Beats, Dramatic Action, Iglesias.

Erving Goffman

KEY TAKEAWAYS

- Goffman saw everyday social life as a kind of theatre.
- He made a clear distinction between people's behaviour in private, behind the scenes, and when others are present.
- He felt that behaviour was powerfully influenced by social status and preserving "face".

Erving Goffman (1922-1982) was a sociologist who studied people's behaviour in social contexts. He wrote many influential works, but there's one that's absolutely fascinating for dramatic thinking. It's called *The Presentation of Self in Everyday Life*, and it deals with the way people behave in front of others and behind the scenes. It's about the idea of impression management, and how we're deeply influenced by the need to present a "face".

Much like Shakespeare, Goffman thought that "all the world's a stage," and that we present ourselves in radically different ways at different times.

Imagine, for example, that you're lolling around on the sofa, with pizza boxes and beer bottles on the floor. It's a comfy Saturday night, and no one is around. Then, suddenly, your boss walks in.

173

This changes everything! Suddenly, you're no longer on your own. And this person has high status. They're important to your life, your job, your future. You wipe your face, hide the beer bottles, switch off the trashy TV, and pull up your sagging tracksuit bottoms.

You switch into "performance" mode.

If a different person arrives, you might start a different performance. Say it's your new lover, for example. You might bar the door until you've thrown your household mess into a cupboard, cleaned your teeth and flung on a fresh top.

Or, if it's your tolerant best friend, you might not bother – though you might still switch into "host" mode and give them a plate and slice of pizza.

For Goffman, human relationships always involve some kind of performance. Our selves and identities aren't static and fixed – they're responsive to context.

So, in your novel or script, the arrival of a new character on the scene will deeply affect the balance of events, and the way that the characters interact. They won't just continue as before. All sorts of new factors, including status and impression management, will suddenly come into play.

When you think about it, many aspects of our lives are performances. We're profoundly influenced by the presence of other people, whether we like it or not. Mostly, we're not even aware of how much we might change.

Goffman takes this theatre metaphor and develops it as a powerful lens for looking at different human interactions.

He studied, for example, how staff in a Highland hotel behaved when no customers were around. They sat differently, spoke differently, and even used cutlery differently.

He looked at territories such as restaurants and commercial spaces, and how they're used by people with different status. He also studied how teams work, and how tensions arise when there isn't a shared group understanding of territorial space.

So, Goffman's thinking chimes deeply with dramatic concepts such as status, space, and tension.

Here are some ideas in *The Presentation of Self in Everyday Life* that might help you with your writing.

Performance Conventions

As social animals, people are in constant negotiation with each other. In most social situations, you'll find widely understood conventions at work. For example, in a shop or restaurant, there are received ideas about the typical relationship between customer and serving staff.

Mostly, these conventions are accepted. But occasionally, people may disrupt the convention, either accidentally, or deliberately. Say, for example, a restaurant customer gets fed up with the slow service, and decides to take matters into their own hands. So they storm into the kitchen, and fill a plate from what's cooking there. There's a clear disruption of the accepted social order.

Life is full of social groups and situations with understood conventions. You'll find them in job interviews, funerals, public services, hotels, schools, and hospitals, just for starters. And they can vary from culture to culture.

In many social situations, there's a lot at stake if the convention is disrupted. Often, these situations are loaded with power relationships. A disruption can topple someone's status, causing a loss of face. Or it can cause the underdog to become suddenly powerful. Say, for example, a maid harassed by a pompous boss wins the lottery, or discovers their embarrassing secret.

These disruptions cause powerful and emotional shifts and reversals in social relations. So they're great for dramatic writing.

TRY THIS:
To power up a scene, look at its underlying social codes. See whether there is an accepted social performance at work, and what its conventions are. For example, there might be a dress code, or expected forms of politeness, or conventional ways

that people sit or stand in relation to each other. There may be conventions around eye contact, physical contact, handling particular objects, or crossing thresholds.

Work out the typical conventions. Now, think about how they might be disrupted. For example, what happens if a patient grabs a doctor's stethoscope? If a customer goes behind the counter?

Goffman describes an interaction between a garage mechanic and a car owner where the motorist wanders behind the scenes and watches, while the mechanics repair his car. The motorist wanted to be part of the backstage action, while the mechanics wanted to work in private. This unsurprisingly caused tension. The motorist then started to handle the spare parts in the workshop, causing yet more tension. Clearly, he misunderstood his social role as a customer.

Look closely at status, and who's in charge in social situations like this. Often, the relationship between customer and service works differently than you might expect. People in service, for example, sometimes have considerable power, and the conventional relationship depends on both sides acknowledging this. To create dramatic tension, find ways to exploit and disrupt the nuances of social codes.

Performance consent

Goffman suggests that a performance is a social construct. For it to work smoothly, both the performers and the audience need to consent to it, and buy into it. If someone is a king, for example, that status needs to be agreed and upheld by common consent. The king needs the courtiers, the subjects - the audience - to sustain his performance as a king.

This tacit agreement between performer and audience underpins many social interactions. And they aren't necessarily about high status or highly public relationships. A shopkeeper needs customers to sustain her performance as a shopkeeper, for example. A spoilt child needs adoring parents to sustain his performance as a spoilt child. A lover needs a partner to sustain a performance as a lover.

These tacit consents can also be disrupted, giving you another option for dramatic tension.

The Emperor's New Clothes is a great example of a story where a performed identity is accepted by others, then disrupted. The King believes his own version of the performance - that he's wearing a suit of gorgeous clothes. The courtiers shore up his performance by accepting the role of sycophantic supporter. Their group behaviour sets up a powerful convention which it would take a strongly rebellious nature to disrupt. Only the small boy, with his naïve, less socialized way of thinking, speaks up, and brings the whole illusion crashing down.

TRY THIS:

Imagine one of your characters adopts higher status behaviour, such as dressing up a notch. Or they gain a higher-status role, such as getting a new job. How is this change accepted by those around them?

Consider whether the character is completely at home in their new role. Maybe they find the change uncomfortable? Maybe they don't quite believe it themselves, and their disbelief "leaks" through in unexpected ways? If, for example, they're trying to eat in an unfamiliar setting, how might their habits stop them managing the impression they want to create?

Or, use this technique the other way round.

For example, an expert might want to perform low expertise, to put people at ease. A professional pastry chef at a family gathering might pretend to love a terrible cake.

What masks might your characters be wearing in different social situations? How important is it that everyone believes the same "truth" about the performance?

What happens if you put a gap between the different beliefs, as in *The Emperor's New Clothes*?

What happens if you play with levels of authenticity and cynicism in different characters?

Front

"Front" is Goffman's term for "equipment" that supports a performance. In theatrical terms, front includes setting, costume, and props.

Setting is a crucial parameter of a performance. People in a courtroom, phone booth, concert hall, hot dog kiosk, church, or someone's home, are typically primed with certain expectations about behaviour – both their own and that of others.

Although we like to think we have freedom to behave as we want, some behaviour is simply more likely or appropriate in each kind of setting. As humans, we're usually good at reading the social conventions, and adapting our behaviour accordingly.

Goffman gives the example of a hearse driver wanting to smoke a cigarette at a funeral. The mourners might accept a driver smoking tactfully out of sight. But they'll be annoyed at a driver who flings a cigarette stub into a bush, in full view of everyone. In an everyday setting, this behaviour would be accepted.

Front can also be established by clothing and furniture. They, too, give social signals. An office suit suggests formality. Wearing make-up suggests a kind of performance. Someone sitting behind a large oak desk is establishing their authority. They impose certain expectations on anyone who walks in.

Mostly, the elements of front are fixed, and don't move around. Settings such as a shop or hospital may imbue characters with a whole sense of meaning, status and identity. This allows you to create conflict by disrupting the relationship between character and front.

178

Imagine, for example, a new factory owner walking in and firing the old one. Or a senior hair stylist arriving to find an apprentice at her chair. How characters interact with the elements of front can be a powerful and economical way of showing their personalities.

Occasionally, front isn't static, but moves around with the character. Goffman mentions the fascinating example of royalty, who carry their performance around with them. They impose it on everyone they meet, through their clothes, ritual objects, and ready audience. From a dramatic perspective, what might happen when the audience doesn't allow this performance?

All these performances are illusions and collusions. They rely on agreement between the participants. They can be upheld and disrupted, to great dramatic effect.

TRY THIS:

Imagine a setting, and brainstorm props and costumes that go to make up its "front". Say, a hairdressing salon, or a garage.

If you could choose only three elements, what would they be? Which elements are essential, and which optional? How attached are the characters to each of these items? If they were spoiled or destroyed, what would happen? What would happen if another character seized these items? Write a scene in which an element of front is disrupted.

Play around with mismatched objects and fronts. For example, a setting with an inappropriate costume, or a costume with an inappropriate prop. Brainstorm ways to explain plausibly how these elements came together. What stories and characters suggest themselves?

179

Team collusion

In Goffman, teams are groups of individuals who collude in a social performance, such as a group of office workers, a school gang, or family members.

For group cohesion and identity, it's important that every member joins in and presents the same face to the "audience". In a restaurant, for example, it would be disloyal for staff to criticize the meals in public.

If someone crosses that unspoken line, it's a very disruptive and powerful statement. For example, when the jeweller Gerald Ratner described his own products as "crap", he destroyed his own company's face. This led to the collapse of his company.

Teams can also be tiny, as in the case of couples. The general assumption is that couples are together out of choice, and can be reasonably be expected to present a loyal face to the wider public. It's extraordinarily uncomfortable to witness someone disrespecting their partner in public. This is used to great effect in dramas such as *Who's Afraid of Virginia Woolf?*

Usually, team allegiance is decided not by someone's personality, but by their social role - receptionist, patient, trainee, etc. However, social roles also come from other contexts - wealth, family background, or another group affiliation.

Sometimes, these different types of status can come into conflict. For example, in military life, a working-class sergeant might have to train an officer from the upper classes. Goffman also mentions the example of maids at a Highland hotel who had a higher status than the owners, because they were daughters of high-status local residents. As a result, the maids behaved deferentially in front of hotel visitors, but dropped the deference when no visitors were around.

Or, a boss might be on informal first name terms with staff when they're on their own, but use formal Mr and Mrs in front of high-status clients.

TRY THIS:

Brainstorm different examples of teams. Think of size, status, nature of connection (work, family, environment, tribe). Imagine who their "audience" might be. Remember that a team can be as few as two people, and an audience as few as one. Are they temporary teams, come together just for this situation? Or are they long-standing and indivisible? What parameters and values unite the members of the team?

TRY THIS:

Explore situations where one team member is at odds with the rest. What line is crossed? What value rejected or disrupted? What changes if an audience witnesses this behaviour?

TRY THIS:

Use "team" thinking to analyze the "team" dynamics of a scene you've already written. Look beyond overt teams to alignments or temporary allegiances. What values do the members share? Do any members shift their loyalty during the scene? How might you use this understanding to strengthen your scene or characters?

Regions

According to Goffman, many settings can be divided into regions where different behaviours take place. As in the theatre, some regions are private or "backstage", and others are public or "front of house".

If you're writing a script or novel, you can play with this distinction to show different facets of your characters, even when no new characters enter the scene to change the status quo.

For example, a restaurant typically has a dining area open to customers, and a kitchen open only to the chefs and waiting staff. There might also be a manager's office where bookings are taken. How might your waiter character behave differently in these distinct regions? What behaviours would be expected, and what would be transgressive or taboo? How might a customer or manager behave in these different regions?

Every shop, factory and public building has similar zones which welcome and exclude different people. They can be explored for distinct, compartmentalized behaviour. Think about what might be disruptive!

The same is also true of our homes. Most of us have a public room which is generally tidy enough to welcome visitors, and a private room which we'd rather not show. Or, we might have taboos around certain regions of the house. Few of us would let random visitors come into the bathroom while we were in the bath, for instance.

All of these regions have implicit behavioural codes that can be upheld or subverted, to add a new dimension to your scenes.

TRY THIS:
Try having a character play against the typical behaviour of a region. Characteristics of "backstage" behaviour mentioned by Goffman include informality, non-standard language, jerkiness, playful aggression, sloppy posture, profanity, whistling and belching. Whereas "front stage" behaviour is the opposite. How does disruptive behaviour affect the characters' relationships? How does it change their power and status?

TRY THIS:
Brainstorm regions for their implicit codes. Explore whether any of your characters are outsiders in the region. Physically speaking, is the backstage region hidden or curtained, or are there barriers? Can the people on one side be seen from the other? Can they all move fluidly between the spaces, or do they have to be invited in? Is there a significant threshold?

TRY THIS:
Explore characters implicitly "unseen" in unusual ways. Goffman mentions the example of Queen Victoria, whose visitors were told to turn the other way when they crossed paths in the garden, so that she didn't have to see them. Waiting staff at high-end restaurants are sometimes "unseen" in this way. How might you play with this convention?

TRY THIS:
Consider how a character's status can shift in different regions. For example, in a glossy car showroom, a mechanic might have lower status than the sales staff. But they might rule the roost in the mechanics' workshop. Even the boss may have to defer to them. Does your scene or chapter allow character status change between two regions?

Audience

Audiences who support the performance of social roles aren't homogenous or static. They shapeshift and cross boundaries. This can create interesting tension.

For example, your character might be known for having a wicked sense of humour with close friends. Maybe they tell outrageous jokes and get everyone falling about in stitches? But in work life, they're a lawyer at a rather stuffy firm. It's a different audience, so they don't let that private side show. But what if a close friend joins the workforce? Might they expect to see the fun side they know and love?

When audiences collide, competing parts of their identity do, too. This can be a good source of dramatic tension.

TRY THIS:
Brainstorm different kinds of audience and their expectations. What happens when you put your characters in front of

different audiences? How might they change? Consider behaviour, language, clothes, status. Now, try mixing the audiences by planting someone from one group in the other - a kind of "cuckoo", if you like. How does this change the dynamics? How does the character feel? What happens if the cuckoo doesn't accept the conventions of the new group?

Impression management

In Goffman's theatre metaphor for everyday life, we are all implicitly actors who try to control the impression we give to others. As soon as an "audience" is around, we adapt our behaviour in subtle and fundamental ways.

Does this mean we're inauthentic or inconsistent? Not at all. Human beings are made up of many different and competing facets which come into play at different times. Only a rare and extraordinary person has bulletproof focus and consistency. In a superhero, these qualities might be fine. But in an ordinary person, they might come across as robotic or megalomaniac!

Or, they're simply very good at "impression management".

Impression management is something politicians and celebrities get very good at. It might be seen as maintaining a kind of mask or disguise, or "keeping up appearances", but that's too simplistic.

The truth is, we all manage impressions to a degree. We may not think we're radically changing our behaviour, but the context around us changes, so we inevitably adapt. That may not mean conformity or compliance. It can mean asserting our own values more forcefully, too. For example, a laidback person who can't stand stuffy gatherings, but is forced to go to one, might become extra-laidback to maintain their own sense of identity.

Nor do people always want to create good impressions, such as coming across as morally upright, or exciting, or powerful. You might be in a dangerous situation where you want to avoid attention. You might prefer to come across as weak, to hide your true strength. You may want to be rebellious and shake up the status quo, and behave in a way that suggests "bad". A gangster might want to keep up a "bad boy" impression, to make sure that everybody fears him.

Understanding the idea of "face" is really powerful for characterisation. It adds a rich layer of complexity and subtext, and can help bring characters fully to life.

TRY THIS:

Take one of your characters and explore the idea of impression management. What impression do they want to give in a particular scene? How might they try to reinforce that impression, whether with behaviour, clothes, what they say, and how they say it? What impression would make them feel vulnerable? Is there any tension between what they show on the outside, and the subtext - how they feel underneath? Look out for moments when the impression shifts. Use this understanding to develop your scene.

TRY THIS:

Look at where your characters stand in relation to impression management. Do any of them have a very clear sense of "face", and try to manage the impression they make very deliberately?

Spies, aspirational characters and people with a traumatic past might have a strong tendency like this. Do any seem entirely consistent, with little difference between their private and various public selves? Do they behave exactly the same, wherever they are? Apart from superheroes, some comedic characters can be like this - Bertie Wooster, for example. Does the importance characters attach to impression management give you potential for conflict?

When you're out and about, observe different settings, and note whether they are front of house or backstage. Notice the transitions between spaces, and how they are signalled - whether with curtains, steps, doorways, or just implicitly. Look out for different regions in the same space, and experience the view from each one. Brainstorm reasons why your characters might go into the different spaces.

TRY THIS:
Go to a place you're familiar with, and ask to gain access to the "backstage" area. How does it feel to be there? What surprises you? What different actions might you take in that space? How does this change your understanding of the front of house area? Write a scene that uses your new understanding.

TRY THIS:
From your work in progress, try writing the same scene in both a front-of-house and a backstage space. How does this affect the behaviour of the characters? How does it affect their status and dynamics? Do the spaces affect the way they speak? Are any of the characters more at home in one space or the other? How does each space affect their degree of cynicism or sincerity?

See also: Space, Status.

Further reading: Goffman, E. (1956) *The Presentation of Self in Everyday Life*. London, Penguin.

Aristotle

KEY TAKEAWAYS

- Aristotle's Poetics is the earliest known book to discuss dramatic structure.
- His concepts have been hugely influential on modern books about story.
- Screenwriting concepts including the hero's journey, fatal flaw, reversal and catharsis are derived from Aristotle's concepts.
- The aim of tragedy was to arouse emotions in the audience, and help them to experience catharsis.

Aristotle was an ancient Greek philosopher who lived from 384-322 BC. He was a pupil of Plato, and tutor to Alexander the Great.

His influence in drama comes from his essay, *Poetics* - the earliest known work on dramatic theory. It sets out many dramatic concepts which are still used today.

It's thought his *Poetics* originally had two parts, dealing with comedy and tragedy. Only the second one, on tragedy, has survived. Aristotle was writing in the fourth century BC, about 100 years after the golden age of ancient Greek theatre, so he was looking back at writers from an earlier time.

Poetics is an overview of what makes a great tragedy. As Aristotle saw it, tragedy had to deal with the lives of great men and women, and show them taking actions with important consequences. Comedy, by contrast, dealt with low status people and their inconsequential lives.

The main purpose of tragedy was to arouse emotions such as pity and fear.

Aristotle outlined six elements of tragedy, and placed them in order of importance. They were, starting with the most important:

PLOT (MYTHOS)
The arrangement of incidents that unfold as a result of the character's nature.

CHARACTER (ETHOS)
Not the people in the play, but the moral quality they represent.

DICTION (LEXIS)
The way the language of the play is spoken by the actors.

THOUGHT (DIANOIA)
Ideas, theme.

SPECTACLE (OPSIS)
The visual aspects of the performance. In Aristotle's view, visual elements were less important than the poetic, though he acknowledged they were emotionally powerful.

MELODY (MELOS)
Choral song - a musical element.

Although ancient Greek drama was a very different art form to today's drama, and it's hard to know exactly what Aristotle's terminology meant in practice, his priorities are interesting for today's writers.

Aristotle prized plot before character qualities. Individual psychology was less important than the actions in the story. In his view, plot should flow logically from a single action (unity of action).

Sometimes, Aristotle is attributed with establishing the three-act structure, but he didn't actually propose this. He just said that good plots present a beginning, middle and end.

That said, he goes into plot in some detail, breaking it down into a kind of typology, including "types of change" and "types of character".

Characters have four types: decent people, noble people, evil people, and in-betweens - the average person.

Plots have two types: a journey from good circumstances to bad, and the inverse, from bad to good.

These plot and character parameters can be combined in different ways, and some make better tragedy than others.

The best kind of plot, according to Aristotle, is one where an average person goes from good fortune to bad, because of an unfortunate error (*hamartia*).

The least tragic plot is when an evil person journeys from bad to good fortune, as this doesn't arouse pity or fear.

Another question for Aristotle is whether the character is innocent about his actions, or knows what he's doing. For example, Oedipus was an innocent, propelled by the hand of fate to sleep with his mother. If he isn't so innocent, what changes?

What's particularly interesting for modern writers is that Aristotle rates a tragedy's success by its effect on the audience, and whether they were emotionally engaged. If they didn't feel pity or fear, or a sense of catharsis, the plot was seen as less successful.

This audience-centric viewpoint is not unlike current research on audience responses to film, and the phenomenology of experiencing stories.

Aristotle's principles have been reworked down the years into influential plot paradigms used by writers today. You'll find them cropping up in Robert McKee's *Story* and Joseph Campbell's *Hero's Journey*, among many others.

Also notable is the fact that Aristotle prized plot and character above the visual and musical aspects of tragedy. They come last in the pecking order of dramatic technique. In his view, they had less to do with the elevated skills of writing and poetry, and more to do with the artisanal skills of production.

Finally, here's a look at some modern plot concepts derived from ideas in Aristotle's *Poetics*.

HAMARTIA

Fatal flaw. *Hamartia* derives from to "miss the mark, to err". In modern terminology, a fatal flaw is the seed that causes a character's downfall, whether ambition, meanness or vanity.

PERIPETEIA

Reversal. *Peripeteia* derives from "sudden change". In drama, it means a reversal of fortune or action, often at the climax of a story. The transformation or transformative arc in a character journey is a type of reversal.

ANAGNORISIS

Recognition. A moment of discovery by the main character, for example, when Oedipus realises who he is.

CATHARSIS

Release of strong emotions. This is covered in *Catharsis*.

MIMESIS

Imitation of the real world. This is covered in *Show and Tell*.

Abraham Maslow

KEY TAKEAWAYS

- Maslow is famous for his description of a "hierarchy of needs" in human psychology.
- Some human needs are more fundamental than others.
- Once basic needs are met, different needs have space to emerge.

Abraham Maslow (1908-1970) was a US psychologist best known for his "hierarchy of needs" - a description of different levels of psychological well-being.

The hierarchy of needs is depicted as a triangle with a broad base, like a pyramid. Basic needs such as warmth and shelter form the broad base of the triangle. Less crucial needs such as self-actualization are at the top.

These needs are useful for dramatic thinking, as they provide a way of looking at characters and what might be driving them.

In Maslow's view, some needs are more important than others for human well-being. People at different levels of the triangle endure different degrees of suffering.

So, for a writer, it's helpful to look at Maslow's hierarchy of needs, to see what it might reveal about characters or themes.

The base of Maslow's triangle is the basic physical needs: food, water, warmth, air, and sex. From a dramatic point of view, these needs are so fundamental that they're powerfully motivating. So, withholding or denying these basic needs will cause your characters problems, and drive their actions.

Next level up in the pyramid is safety. This might take the form of shelter or security, such as your home or refuge. Or, it might mean security of resources, such as money, property, or your health. Characters who lack safety are likely to be anxious or unrooted, and on a quest to find it in some form.

Next in the hierarchy is the need for love and belonging. Once our basic needs are met, we have time and space to prioritize social connections - friends, family, tribe, or anyone who validates us and makes us feel worthy and wanted.

Characters without love or membership of a group may be driven to seek it. Rejected characters may want to find an alternative tribe where they're accepted. The drive to be part of a social group is incredibly strong. It's bound up in our identity and sense of self. Without it, we can struggle to maintain our sense of worth.

Another important aspect of love and belonging is intimacy, whether sexual or emotional. Closeness to others helps us to feel bonded and wanted, as well as being physically grounding.

Further up the hierarchy is a more active form of love: esteem and respect from others. Love and belonging can come from familiarity or tolerance, but esteem is an active choice, and having esteem gives us a strong sense of validation, confidence and dignity.

Characters who are looked down on and despised will struggle, even if their other needs are met.

As mammals, we all have a place in the mammal equivalent of the pecking order, and this profoundly affects our interactions and choices. So, explore how and whether your characters are held in esteem, and who respects them. Esteem might not be a marker of goodness or morality. For example, a murderous mafia boss may be hugely respected by his sidekicks.

Most of these needs are "deficiency needs" - something we lack and therefore seek. But at the top of the pyramid, there's a further level, towards positive growth. Here, you find self-actualization: the desire to make the best of yourself, personal growth, and peak experiences, such as awe and ecstasy.

Maslow's theory was that people are motivated by different needs at different levels, and the lower levels in the pyramid need to be addressed first.

If you need food or shelter, you're unlikely to be motivated by morals or creativity. If you need companionship first and foremost, it doesn't matter whether you're held in great esteem.

I find this a useful lens for looking at characters, and what might be driving them. It shows how some wants and desires are more important than others, and will usurp others in the hierarchy. For example, someone who is freezing with cold won't be interested in how they appear to others. Someone who has lost all dignity won't be worried about self-actualization.

The basic biological needs are linked to high stakes. People without air, heat, food or shelter will die. And if no one can have sex, the whole of humanity will die out. In these situations, people don't have the luxury of thinking about self-actualization or self-improvement.

If you're writing a scene, look at where the different characters sit in the hierarchy of needs. Are they far apart? How does this affect their interaction? If they're close together, this can be interesting dramatically, as they may have their sights on the same thing - that prize, or goal, or loaf of bread.

Screenwriters sometimes explore the difference between what characters want, and what they *really* want. To put it another way, what they think they want, and what they truly *need*.

For example, your character may covet a beautiful sports car beyond all else, but what they really need is a sense of their own self-worth, which they might get from a truly loving relationship. Sometimes, physical objects are totems for something deeper,

and Maslow's hierarchy of needs helps to highlight what might
be really going on.

TRY THIS:
Watch a scene from a film or read a book that you love.
Where do the characters sit on the hierarchy of needs? How
sympathetic do you feel towards them? What happens if you
change an element of the mix, particularly using a different
level in the hierarchy? What happens to the character
dynamics? Is there a point in the story where their most
pressing need is met? Now, look at a scene from your work in
progress. Identify what needs the character has, and whether
they'll be met during the story.

TRY THIS:
Explore deficiency needs (lack of something) and self-
actualization needs (striving for something) in one of your
characters. What's to be gained, and what's at stake, if they
don't get what they need? Is there a difference between what
they want, and what they truly need? What unmet needs do you
care most about? If you had to give up something from each
level of Maslow's hierarchy, what would it be? What about
your characters? Free-write some of your thoughts, and see
what you discover about your themes.

See also: Status, Wants and Stakes.

Karl Iglesias

KEY TAKEAWAYS

- Iglesias believes scriptwriting is the business of emotion delivery.
- He discusses how audiences experience films moment by moment.
- He offers Hollywood examples of emotion-driven storytelling.
- He dives into techniques for creating different kinds of emotions.

Karl Iglesias is a US screenwriter, script doctor and teacher who focuses on how to write emotion. He says that Hollywood movies are in the business of "emotion delivery", and that the audience's emotional experience should be the primary consideration for scriptwriters.

His book, *Writing for Emotional Impact*, looks at advanced dramatic techniques for attracting and engaging audiences. It's essentially a phenomenological take on screenwriting. That is, it looks at screenwriting through the lens of the audience's lived experience.

This book is well worth adding to your dramatic writing library, as it includes a great deal of detail and specifics about the different kinds of emotions, and ways of keeping an audience engaged. I found it really refreshing because it puts the audience first, and provides a welcome alternative to the traditional plot-driven and character-driven approaches.

Here's an overview of Iglesias' thinking, and some of the techniques I found particularly useful. As he says, it's a "smorgasbord" of techniques, but the common thread is audience engagement of different kinds, harnessing our natural impulses of curiosity, empathy, and desire.

Iglesias says it's important to be aware that the first person who will read your script professionally isn't a director, producer or anyone high up in the screen industry. It's far more likely to be a poorly paid film graduate in an entry-level position who is trying to gain a foothold in the industry.

These readers are extremely film literate, and want to be woken up and riveted by what they see on the page. They want to forget that they're reading a screenplay as a job, and be immersed in the world of the story.

You need to engage these demanding readers right away.

"Concept is the core of script. Concept sells"

The key emotion to aim for here is: compelling.

Does the idea compel the audience to buy a ticket to the film? Will it interest people enough to have box office success?

It has to stand out as an idea that will get people's ears pricking up, so that they go and see the film. Any script idea needs that marketability right from the start.

So, if your core idea isn't "high concept", with instant and sizeable appeal, then you need to work on it at the idea stage, and build that quality in.

What's more, for broad appeal, the idea can't be so original and "out there" that general audiences switch off. You're looking for a sweet spot between originality and familiarity.

Iglesias offers a number of techniques for increasing your idea's appeal, such as pushing extremes, the worst thing that can happen to your character, time limits, and setting the story in a unique world. Your idea also needs to offer conflict, and something important at stake.

This thinking has a lot in common with dramatic technique, where you're looking to amp up the conflict and tension, and raise the stakes for the characters. Spectacle also comes into it – the appeal of an interesting and distinctive world to set your story in.

But a compelling concept isn't enough. You also need an underlying theme that your audience can invest in.

Theme

Theme is complex to grasp, but without it, the script can feel empty. Theme is the reason why your story matters. It's the point of your story.

However, if you're too heavy-handed about theme, it can come across as preachy. If you ever find your characters speaking a message, take stock, and see if you can express it in another way.

Iglesias suggests categories of themes which are universal, and resonate deeply with most people. They include:

- Separation-reunion themes, such as "the underdog triumphs".
- Humanity in jeopardy themes such as "good versus evil", "revenge".
- Relationship themes, such as "love gained or lost", "dangerous attraction of friendship".

To discover your themes, Iglesias suggests looking for emotional indignation - topics that make your blood boil, and values that are important to you.

Rather than formulating a premise, turn the theme into a question that you're exploring through your characters. For example, "can love survive death?" Then dramatize this question. Show it through your characters' actions (see *Show and Tell*).

One powerful way to explore the question of the theme is through the protagonist and antagonist. These two characters on opposite sides can reveal contrasting facets of the theme, and show its complexity and richness. Subplot characters can also reveal different layers and facets in a similar way.

Character

Iglesias usefully breaks down character development into five main questions which link to other sections in this book.

The questions are:

1. Who is my main character? (See *Dramatic Action, Secrets*)
2. What does my character want? (See *Wants and Stakes, Stanislavski*)
3. Why do they want it? (See *Wants and Stakes*)
4. What happens if they fail? (See *Fatal Flaw, Wants and Stakes*)
5. How do they change? (See *Transformation, Marks*).

But what makes audiences connect to characters? Iglesias identifies three basic ways:

Recognition

This taps into our emotions of understanding and empathy. If we see characters with familiar values and emotions, we can identify with them, and experience their story vicariously.

So, find ways to show your characters experiencing familiar emotions.

Fascination

You can also engage an audience by piquing their interest in different ways. People are interested in things that are novel and unique, so see what fresh angles you can bring to the table. Script readers are looking for something they haven't seen before.

Paradoxical and contradictory characters are also intriguing - say, an evil character with a secret weakness, or someone with unexpected flaws and emotional wounds that hold them back. Let your characters surprise you.

Mystery

Mystery harnesses our sense of curiosity and anticipation. Mysteries can be about the past, the present or the future, so brainstorm different scenarios and see what can enrich your characters' lives. Maybe they have a secret that haunts them? Or maybe we're following them as they uncover a mystery in their world?

Other techniques for character empathy

We care about victims – people we feel sorry for, whether through misfortune, betrayal, exclusion, or other reasons.

We care about characters showing humanity – people who are liked by children and animals, show forgiveness, or risk their lives for a cause for others.

We care about characters with desirable qualities, such as power, glamour, courage, rebelliousness, or passion.

Thinking about your characters, what reasons do they give an audience to care about them? Can you give them more layers?" "Patting the dog" to show a character's likeability is a common screenwriting trope, so you may want to dig deeper for a fresh angle.

Story

For Iglesias, the most essential reader emotion is interest. The opposite of interest is boredom, and for a storyteller, that's a sin.

Interest is an overarching emotion which includes fascination, insight and awe. Other important elements of the toolkit are conflict and originality. However, even more important for interest is a sense of change.

As Iglesias says, "every story, every scene, and every beat is about to change". If situations aren't changing, the story gets dull. Important types of change include discoveries (changes in knowledge), and decisions (changes in actions).

Check your story to see if there's enough change, conflict, and escalation to keep things interesting.

Curiosity

For screenwriters, questions are a powerful structuring device. Not only does your story need a central dramatic question, but each scene and sequence also needs a question, to keep your audience interested. Iglesias describes a question as an emotional itch that needs to be scratched - a powerful driver.

However, questions need to be carefully chosen and controlled. If you have too many unanswered questions, the audience can get confused.

Does your script have a central dramatic question? Does each scene have a question? What's keeping the audience interested at each point in the story?

Anticipation/hope/fear

If your characters are looking ahead to something in the future, your audience, too, will be interested in seeing what happens. This could be something positive such as a happy surprise, or something negative, such as a warning, or a bomb about to go off. These future events can be planted in the script, to create anticipation.

Dramatic irony creates a powerful form of anticipation, as it puts the reader in a superior position where they know more than the characters (see *Dramatic Irony*).

Suspense

Suspense comes with a sense of tension and anxiety. It's linked to situations that are unpredictable. If your script is too predictable, it will lose the audience.

Alfred Hitchcock famously defined an important distinction between suspense and surprise.

"Surprise" is when something unexpected happens suddenly. Say, a bomb going off under the table.

"Suspense" is knowing about the bomb and feeling the growing tension as it ticks down. Hitchcock said that suspense was much

201

more powerful and prolonged than the momentary impact of surprise. So it's fundamental to good storytelling.

With all these forms of anticipation, you're controlling a careful balance between frustration and reward. If the character always gets what they want (or doesn't), the pattern gets predictable.

With tension, you need to ring the changes, and release it from time to time. Be aware of what you want your audience to feel, and hit different emotional notes.

Structure

Iglesias views story structure through the lens of emotions. Act One corresponds to attraction. Act Two corresponds to tension and anticipation. Act Three corresponds to satisfaction.

Endings are particularly important, because they're the final emotional impact your audience is left with. Consider how you want them to feel when the story ends. Do you need a happy, tragic, bittersweet, twist or open ending?

One fascinating aspect of Iglesias' book is the concept of the "emotional palette". This is analogous to the painter's palette. Ideally, to build an interesting scene, you need to vary the emotional tones experienced by the reader, whether curiosity, anger, fear, or joy.

If you get the book - and I highly recommend it – you get a free copy of *The Emotional Thesaurus*, which gathers together emotions by type and intensity level. This is a really helpful tool for thinking about escalation and rising tension.

Other powerful techniques for emotional impact

* Use high-energy verbs (*clangs* instead of *rings*, *sobs* instead of *cries*, *strides* instead of *walks*).

202

- Use sensory words to appeal to the different senses (*slap, tattered, billows, musky*).
- Use sound words (onomatopoeia) to bring noises to life (*crash, squish, tick*).
- Use adjectives with emotional resonance (*dingy, busy, silent, tacky*).

Writng for Emotional Impact also has a valuable section on dialogue techniques which ties in well with the chapter in this book on *Beats*.

TRY THIS:

Choose a scene and draw a line representing its emotional intensity, its peaks and troughs.

Think about what you want the audience to feel at each point. Where does the emotional impact on the audience rise and fall? What's the emotion you want them to feel?

Have you aimed for different notes on the emotional palette, or have you simply written variations on similar emotions, such as fear or anxiety? Do you have enough moments of change to sustain interest?

TRY THIS:

Map your story shape based on what you want the audience to feel at each moment.

Do you have a variety of notes? Where can you clarify and heighten the key emotion?

Identify any places where the characters are talking about their emotions, rather than evoking those emotions in the audience. Actors often say that audiences disengage from characters who show too much emotion. Try the effect of cutting back on overt emotion.

TRY THIS:

Watch a favourite film and note down the different emotions you experience, marking their intensity on a 1 to 10 scale.

Looking at each emotion in turn, brainstorm different ways of evoking them.

Are any of the emotions more difficult for you to write about than others? Which ones are more natural to you? Write some scenes of your own to expand your emotional palette.

See also: Stakes, Contrasts, Dramatic Irony, Beats.

Dara Marks

KEY TAKEAWAYS

- Marks' big idea is the "transformational arc" in story structure.
- In her view, the defining feature of story is the character's internal change.
- She offers a holistic alternative to story structure driven by plot.

Dara Marks is a US script consultant and teacher. Her book *Inside Story: The Power of the Transformational Arc* is a meaty look at story structure through the specific lens of character change.

I found this particularly helpful, as it crystallized for me why some stories don't feel meaningful, while others do. Put simply: if the main character doesn't transform from one state to another, nothing has really happened. There may be plenty of spectacle, activity and events, but a deep emotional core may be missing.

I read a lot of work in progress, and this is a very common issue. So often, stories are linear - not chronologically, but with a straight escalating structure, without any real pivot or transformation for the character. Marks has helped me to understand this fundamental.

For me, a straight story shape is structurally more like an anecdote or report. It's just a sequence of escalating events. For a story to have a thematic point, and therefore emotional power, it needs a knotty, pivotal moment when the protagonist changes.

This is sometimes known as a "reversal" or, for the ancient Greeks, *peripeteia*. A reversal can happen at a climactic point in the story arc, as well as within scenes.

The ancient Greeks saw *peripeteia* as a change of fortune - that is, the unavoidable hand of fate. But in modern dramaturgy, change is ascribed to personal growth from deep within the character.

Like Stanislavski and Iglesias, Marks is interested in the inner lives of characters, and the audience's experiences of their emotional journey by proxy. Her work is also aligned to Jung and to Vogler's *Hero's Journey*, which has a similar structure to the transformational arc.

However, her terminology is different because it derives from lived emotions in process, rather than a heroic quest. So, it's a useful alternative perspective.

Broadly, the transformational arc in a story proceeds:

- from the unknown to the known
- from resistance to release
- from awakening to enlightenment, to a quasi-death experience, to renewal.

These elements map onto features you may already be familiar with from other screenwriting books, such as the inciting incident, rising action, climax, and act two turning-point.

At the turning-point, the protagonist has to choose between turning back, or pushing through, facing down opposition, and emerging as a changed person.

But this isn't just a mechanical process. The character is on a profound emotional journey from one state to another. Their transformation is like an awakening or renewal, which may be for good (*Little Red Riding Hood*) or for ill (*The Portrait of Dorian Gray*).

If you're into studying the nitty-gritty of story structure, and have enjoyed the detail of Robert McKee's *Story*, then you'll get a lot from *Inside Story*.

But even if all you absorb is the need for a powerful transformational moment at the heart of your story, it'll still transform the impact of your writing.

TRY THIS:

Find the mid-point of your story. Does it have a true character transformation, where your protagonist takes a major, life-changing decision? Or does it simply escalate in a linear way?

Try mapping the emotional journey in a simplified way, using "from... to" or "before... after", to find its two narrative poles.

Are the polarities clear? Does the transformational moment feel decisive, like a pivot, or is it muddy?

Does the beginning/end or before/after highlight a clear theme, such as "good/evil always wins" or "be careful what you wish for?"

Note that not every story has a transformational arc, and other structures are possible. See the section on *Fatal Flaw* and check out *Alternative Scriptwriting* by Jeff Rush and Ken Dancyger.

TRY THIS:

Analyze well-known fairy tales to identify their main characters' transformational arcs.

For example, Little Red Riding Hood transitions from innocence to experience. Cinderella transitions from lowly and rejected to celebrated and admired.

Identify any moral messages implied by the story structure.

Explore what you'd feel about the story if you were denied the expected transformation.

See also: Transformation, Fatal Flaw, Stanislavski, Iglesias.

Gaston Bachelard

KEY TAKEAWAYS

- Bachelard applied psychological thinking to physical spaces, such as rooms and mountains.
- He identified spatial archetypes and their psychological impacts.
- His spatial archetypes can help writers to think more boldly about the effect of setting.

Gaston Bachelard was a French philosopher. His influential book *The Poetics of Space* was written in the 1950s.

It's a far from easy read, as it's often abstract and poetic. However, some of Bachelard's thinking about spaces is fascinating for storytelling.

I've pulled together some of the main ideas I took from his book here. If you read the whole book, I suggest you take it slowly and savour it, as you might a book of poetry. I found it absolutely transformative for my thinking about space, and spatial dynamics.

One of Bachelard's key ideas is that spaces have certain archetypal qualities. For example, the Nest, the Mountain and the Drawer are clearly different shapes and sizes of physical space, but they're also different conceptually and poetically.

208

A Nest, for example, is enclosed and protected. A Mountain is high, wild and open. Bachelard only looks at a number of representative spaces, but you can think in this archetypal way about any kind of space you are interested in. For example, what's the essence of a Prison? Of an Attic? Of a Wardrobe?

Note that although Bachelard doesn't write these spaces with capital letters, it can be helpful to think of them that way. In his thinking, they have a heightened and transcendent quality that goes beyond their literal meaning.

TRY THIS:

Look at your scenes, and think about their archetypal setting. If you can't align their setting to a clear type of space, it may be that the central idea of your setting is muddy, and could be sharpened up.

In Shakespeare's plays, the stage directions often indicate spaces that are a clear, succinct microcosm.

A heath – wild, open, high.
A room of state in the castle – enclosed, imposing, grand.
A churchyard – quiet, earth, graveside.

These spaces are particular and familiar enough to evoke a clear picture in our heads. And yet they also feel universal, as though they could stand in for any heath, room of state or churchyard, anywhere in the world. So, they have a metaphorical and poetic weight, too, which makes them powerfully evocative.

In your settings, it's a good idea to strive for this same kind of clarity.

This doesn't necessarily mean filling your set with lots of detail. On the contrary, it means distil its general, broad-brush meaning.

Imagine someone from another country or culture seeing your archetypal space. Would they understand its general nature, feelings, restrictions, opportunities and interactions? Would they physically behave or interact with it in a broadly similar way? If you took language away, would it read clearly?

To understand the potency and transferability of this kind of spatial thinking, think about stage plays you may have seen, and images from famous plays. For example, Samuel Beckett's Waiting for Godot takes place in a mysterious open space with a tree. However the play is produced, in different countries and contexts, its world is instantly recognisable.

Similarly, *Shakespeare's Romeo and Juliet* has a famous balcony scene. The Balcony is a place of escape, longing and love, and, again, paints a picture in our minds which travels across language and culture.

So, see if you can imagine your own settings as quintessential spaces like this. If a scene feels underpowered, try reimagining it in a different space, with different resonances.

Try reducing the detail needed to create the space. If you had to create it on stage with minimal means, what would be absolutely necessary? For example, you might invoke an entire prison with only some bars. For fiction writing, this suggests that bars, more than any other element in the setting, need to be clearly written, to evoke a strong picture in the reader's mind.

And Bachelard goes further in his thinking about archetypal or "poetic" spaces. He suggests that they correlate with spaces in our inner landscapes or mental maps. His spatial archetypes are psychological and metaphorical spaces, as well as literal. Bachelard suggests that they may be independent of culture, relatively consistent, and a primal part of the human experience.

For example, the Cellar evokes dark, buried mysteries, while the Attic suggests discovery, and an ascension away from the core of the house. The Shell is a sheltered safe space which is nomadic, and can be carried around, allowing us to carry our sense of security with us.

Although this correlation of physical spaces to mental landscapes may seem fanciful, Bachelard took a strong interest in architecture, where the impact of spaces on how people feel (the phenomenology of spaces) is well recognised.

So, when thinking about your characters, it's worth considering how the space they're in aligns with what they feel. Can they easily feel joy and revelation in a cellar? Safety on a mountain top? What thresholds do they cross? How can you heighten the use of spaces to give your settings a more powerful impact?

SOME SPACES EXPLORED BY BACHELARD

The House
The Cellar
The Garret
Drawers, Chests and Wardrobes
Nests
Shells
Corners

OTHER SPACES TO EXPLORE

The Forest
The Sea Shore
The Kitchen
The Hill
The Road

TRY THIS:

Explore iconic spaces you've seen in films or books. Is a spatial archetype at work? What elements are crucial to the impact of the scene? What can be left out?

How does the space make the characters feel? What changes when they leave the space?

What's beyond the space?

TRY THIS:

Explore different spatial parameters: inside/outside; up/down; enclosed/open; large/small; wide/narrow; high/low; hidden/revealed.

How does each parameter change the potential of the space? What different dramatic actions become possible, if you move the characters to the other dimension?

See also: Space, Scene.

Keith Johnstone

KEY TAKEAWAYS

- Johnstone is influential for his teaching of improvisation techniques.
- Improv is an extreme state of acceptance and openness.
- Improv techniques can help to harness the power of the subconscious.

Keith Johnstone is an extraordinary British-Canadian theatre practitioner and playwright who specializes in improvisation. He developed Theatre Sports, a form of improvised theatre, and the Impro System of improvisation training. His books, *Impro: Improvisation and the Theatre,* and *Impro for Storytellers* are an amazing source of inspiration for writers, as well as being an engaging and often hilarious read.

You can see some of his work online, including a TEDx Talk called *Don't Be Prepared,* which is online here:

https://www.youtube.com/watch?time_continue= 10&v=bz9mo4qW9bc

Johnstone was motivated by a feeling that school stifled his imagination. When he became a drama teacher, he decided to encourage spontaneity by reversing all that he had been taught.

213

Many improv techniques are helpful for dramatic technique. The main underlying ethos is one of generosity and acceptance. The performers make "offers" which are accepted and developed, to move the scene forward.

An "offer" is a suggestion made by one improviser to the others. For example, one might say, "is that a blizzard up ahead?" In everyday conversation, you might close this down with a contrary suggestion: "No. You're seeing things/ it's sunny/ your eyesight/a flurry of feathers".

In impro, the other improvisers would accept this suggestion, and build on it. Their aim is not to be clever and top someone's suggestion, but simply to accept it, and incorporate it into the scene.

Often, in beginner scripts, I see a lot of "closing down" between characters. One character may be dominant, and constantly assert power over the other, by saying "no", or rejecting suggestions, or diverting the conversation.

Sometimes, this is because of a false understanding of the nature of conflict. A writer may think that, to introduce conflict into their scene, the characters need to be categorically against each other, and clearly express that disagreement in words.

However, conflict is usually more subtle than this, and tension can be created in other ways. One way is the delicious tension of not knowing what will happen next. Another is seeing an unknown story unfold before your eyes - the very act of creation. I've seen improv described as the place where fear meets joy, which seems apt.

Here are just a few of the insights I've drawn from Johnstone's work. I really recommend you read his books in full.

- ❋ Characters don't always need to be in conflict. There's great audience enjoyment and energy from seeing characters collude in a responsive way, their joint action unfolding before our eyes. It can be tremendously exciting to see the creative process in dynamic action.

❋ Extreme generosity is as dynamic as extreme conflict. Saying "yes" can throw things wide open and open unknown possibilities. Sometimes, this freedom is far scarier than obstacles and boundaries.

❋ As an analytical and editorial type of writer, I tend to question and narrow down options. It's tremendously challenging to be invited to do the opposite.

❋ People find it hard to invent stories. Instead, try thinking of interrupting routines. If your characters normally live in a street and take the bus into town, imagine disruptions to that routine. That might be the start of a story.

See also: Improv.

Bibliography

If you'd like to dig deeper into dramatic techniques and thinkers, check out these books. Most of them aren't an easy read! But they're well worth dipping into for inspiration and further research.

Aristotle (2013) Poetics. Oxford, Oxford University Press.

Bachelard, G. (1958) The Poetics of Space. London, Penguin.

Caldarone, M. and Lloyd-Williams, M. (2017) *Actions: The Actors' Thesaurus*. London, Nick Hern.

Dancyger, K. and Rush, J. (2002) *Alternative Scriptwriting. Successfully Breaking the Rules*. London, Routledge.

Geary, J. (2011) *I Is an Other: The Secret Life of Metaphor and How it Shapes the Way We See the World*. London, Harper Collins.

Goffman, E. (1956) *The Presentation of Self in Everyday Life*. London, Penguin.

Hammond, W. and Steward, D. (eds) (2008) *Verbatim Verbatim: Contemporary Documentary Theatre*. London, Oberon Books.

Iglesias, K. (2011) *Writing for Emotional Impact*. Livermore, WingSpan Publishing.

Johnstone, K. (1979) *Impro: Improvisation and the Theatre*. London, Bloomsbury.

Marks, D. (2007) *Inside Story: The Power of the Transformational Arc*. Three Mountains Press.

Stanislavski, C. (2013) *An Actor Prepares*. London, Bloomsbury Academic.

PART III

And Finally...

I hope you've enjoyed this overview of the main dramatic techniques, and found some useful nuggets to put to work in your own writing. I'm still discovering something new every day! Sign up for my Method Writing mailing list if you'd like to know more.

WHAT'S NEXT?
I've love a review! Just a quick comment makes all the difference, as you'll know if you're an author or publisher yourself. Thanks so much!

JOIN METHOD WRITING NEWSLETTER
For more pro writing tips and a free ebook, *Copywriting for Creative Writers*, join my Method Writing VIP CLUB: www.method-writing.com/vip-club/

KEEP IN TOUCH
You can contact me via info@method-writing.com or via Facebook, Twitter, Instagram or www.method-writing.com.

About Jules Horne

I come from the Borders of Scotland, home of the Border ballads, so unsurprisingly I've grown up with a Gothic imagination and a gene for storytelling. I write fiction and plays which have been on stage and on BBC Radio, and perform spoken word as Rebel Cello. I teach on the MA in Creative Writing with the Open University, and co-wrote the Script strand.

Join my mailing list at www.method-writing.com to get tips and advice on advanced writing craft. I'm an independent author so I'd really appreciate your book review online!

221

Method Writing Books

METHOD WRITING FREE BLUEPRINT:

Copywriting for Creative Writers

Interested in starting a freelance writing business? This free ebook is packed with practical advice for creative writers, journalists, marketers and bloggers.

To get your free ebook, join the Method Writing mailing list:

www.method-writing.com

METHOD WRITING BOOK 1:

How to Launch a Freelance Copywriting Business

ISBN: 978-0-9934354-5-4 (paperback)
ISBN: 978-0-9934354-4-7 (ebook)
ISBN: 978-1-9164960-3-3 (audiobook)

Want to get started as a freelance commercial writer for hire? This practical guide gives you the business skills you need to put your words to work.

"Wish I'd had this book years ago!"

Babs, journalism teacher

"A Godsend for me... a clear, comprehensive, friendly and approachable down-to-earth manual. Highly recommended."

Malcolm Pryce, novelist

"Digs deep into the nitty-gritty of the copywriting profession."

Claire, novelist and publishing scout

I felt I had the necessary skills to start my own freelance copywriting business but I didn't really know how to get things up and running. There are a lot of courses and 'gurus' on the subject out there, but among an overload of information, it's hard to pin down what is actually useful and relevant. Jules' book was all I needed. It cut to the chase and provided me with all the information, advice, and tips I needed to launch. Within days of following her advice, I was landing clients and earning money as my own boss, in charge of my own time. Re-reads have also helped me stay on track.

Ben Robinson, Red Robin Copywriting

METHOD WRITING BOOK 3:

Writing for Audiobooks

ISBN: 978-1-9164960-1-9 (paperback)

ISBN: 978-1-9164960-0-2 (ebook)

ISBN: 978-1-9164960-2-6 (audiobook)

Are you an author interested in audiobooks? Want to get your fiction or non-fiction book ready for the fastest-growing publishing market? Voice-first writing skills are a must if you want to make your book really shine on the audio platform.

Whether you're an author, publisher, narrator, or preparing your own book for voiceover narration, *Writing for Audiobooks* will get you audio-ready! Pack with radio writing advice for fiction, non-fiction and scripts.

"Audiobooks are the fastest-growing segment in publishing, but writing for audio first is a skill that few writers have needed to learn. Until now. If you want to make sure your writing resonates for this growing audience, Jules's book will give you useful tips for adjusting your words and reaching listeners. Highly recommended!"
Joanna Penn, The Creative Penn

Excerpt from *Writing for Audiobooks*

Audiobooks are enjoying an exciting boom, and it's set to continue and grow.

More and more people are listening to audiobooks in preference to reading. Major publishers are reporting 20-30% increases in audiobook sales. And some are commissioning straight-to-audio fiction.

So if you're a writer, this is a big deal. The book market is shifting towards audio, and you need to be part of it.

However, not every book is great for audio. Not every writer knows about audio writing techniques. Those that do will find their books make an easy transition. The writing will be more fun for narrators to read, and clearer and more compelling for listeners to hear.

Writing for the ear calls for specific skills. Skills that are well known in the worlds of radio, performance, and spoken word. But far less familiar in the world of traditional books.

Since audiobooks are on the rise, it makes sense for writers to learn those skills, and soon.

I'm particularly excited because I'm a fiction writer with a professional background in radio. I've written for stage, and performed spoken word in English and Scots. The rhythms and music of spoken word are in my writing DNA anyway.

And suddenly, the extra techniques I've learned from radio and stage writing have turned out to be very useful indeed.

They're easy to learn, and they'll transform your impact as an audiobook author.

You may even decide to join the many authors now writing with audio-first in mind.

This is a handbook for anyone interested in audio writing – writing for the ear, writing for performance.

If you're traditionally published, you'll learn audio writing strategies and be well prepared for this growing and lucrative market.

If you're an indie author, you'll learn how to prepare your books for audio recording and what to consider when working with a narrator or narrating your own book.

I'll be covering, among other things:

- How do you write for the audio platform?
- What's different about writing for the ear, rather than the eye?
- How do you deal with visual elements such as URLs, images, graphs, tables, headers?
- Can audio-first writing improve your book for listeners?

The answer is "yes". Of course!

The written and spoken word are very different media, as you'll discover. And audio is tremendous fun!

SO, WHO'S THIS BOOK FOR?

Anyone who wants to up their writing game, and polish their books for better audio impact.

Fiction authors – both traditionally published and indie – who are interested in this booming market for storytellers.

Non-fiction authors wondering how to adapt their books for audio.

Teachers of professional writing who want an overview of audio-specific writing skills.

Early adopters excited by audiobooks. Hopefully, that's you!

But first, a story.

I was a young, newly published fiction writer. I'd even won a prize and was feeling pretty pleased with myself. And I'd just written my first playscript, and was in my first rehearsal, waiting for my beautiful words to be beautifully read by actors.

So I was shocked by what happened next.

The actors – very experienced and one even rather famous – were running out of breath. My lines were too long. Full of qualifying clauses. Piled-on adjectives. Some bits weren't even quite logical.

Now, I'd worked very hard on that script. It was well written, and well edited. But as a script for performance, it didn't work.

Wow - did I sharpen up after that! Every word had to be weighed and counted.

An audiobook is a script. Your narrator makes it a performance. And that alone calls for different writing skills.

So, some of what follows comes from the world of performance. Some of it comes from my BBC training in radio news. Some of it comes from teaching many aspiring and inspiring writers as a tutor for the Open University.

Most of the techniques are straightforward, and you can put them into practice right away. I've gathered some of the main ones in a download on my website – see the link at the end of this book.

Others go deeper into what's different about ears, linear thinking and audio flow – including hooks and arcs that keep things moving forward.

Rest assured: you don't need to change your writing voice – simply get some extra editing and structuring skills to help listeners who'll hear your story only once. Skills that are great, as it happens, for your editing in general.

Audio offers an amazing sense of connection. The intimacy of voices in your ear, the music, rhythm and humanity of different and distinctive ways of telling stories.

You may find that the spoken word is more natural for you, and your writing can flourish in audio form.

If you already write spoken word, performance poetry, dialect or scripts, maybe audiobooks are your natural home!

Audio is different.

Publishers, readers and writers are just beginning to discover its full potential.

It's a fascinating time, and exciting to be part of it....

WANT TO READ MORE?

Get *Writing for Audiobooks* from Amazon,
Barnes & Noble and all good bookstores.

INTERESTED IN NEWS ABOUT FORTHCOMING BOOKS?

Sign up for the Method Writing VIP club:

www.method-writing.com

Printed in Great Britain
by Amazon